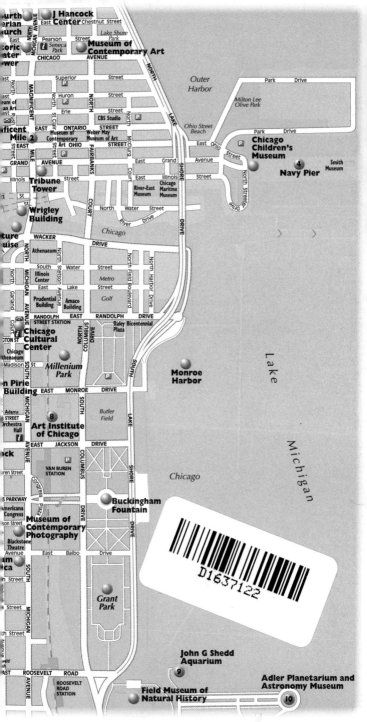

Fodor's

Chicago's
25Best

by Mick Sinclair

Fodor's Travel Publications
New York • Toronto •
London • Sydney • Auckland
www.fodors.com

How to Use This Book

KEY TO SYMBOLS

✚	Map reference to the accompanying fold-out map
✉	Address
☎	Telephone number
🕐	Opening/closing times
🍴	Restaurant or café
🚆	Nearest rail station
Ⓜ	Nearest subway (Metro) station
🚍	Nearest bus route
⛴	Nearest riverboat or ferry stop
♿	Facilities for visitors with disabilities

❓	Other practical information
▷	Further information
ℹ	Tourist information
✋	Admission charges: Expensive (over $9), Moderate ($3–$9), and Inexpensive ($2 or less)
★	Major Sight
★	Minor Sight
👣	Walks
🚌	Excursions
🏬	Shops
🎵	Entertainment and Nightlife
🍴	Restaurants

This guide is divided into four sections

• **Essential Chicago:** an introduction to the city and tips on making the most of your stay.

• **Chicago by Area:** We've broken the city into five areas, and recommended the best sights, shops, entertainment venues, nightlife and restaurants in each one. Suggested walks help you to explore on foot.

• **Where to Stay:** the best hotels, whether you're looking for luxury, budget or something in between.

• **Need to Know:** The info you need to make your trip run smoothly, including getting about by public transportation, weather tips, emergency phone numbers and useful websites.

Navigation In the Chicago by Area chapter, we've given each area its own color, which is also used on the locator maps throughout the book and the map on the inside front cover.

Maps The fold-out map accompanying this book is a comprehensive street plan of Chicago. The grid on this fold-out map is the same as the grid on the locator maps within the book. We've given grid references within the book for each sight and listing.

Contents

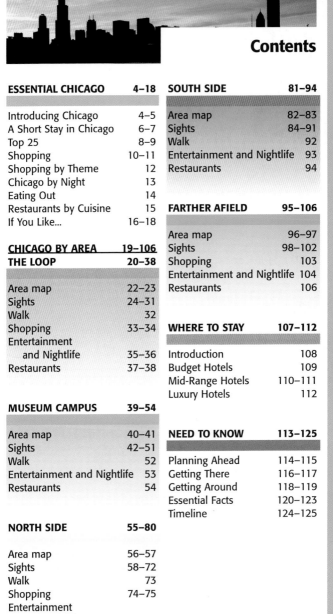

CONTENTS

Introducing Chicago

Poet Carl Sandburg called it "City of the big shoulders." Mayor Richard J. Daley boasts it's "the city that works." Pick your interpretation—city of brawn and industry, brash and bustling, modern and innovative—it's all here in Chicago.

The unofficial capital of the Midwest, Chicago earned the moniker "Second City" for trailing New York in size. But Chicago never played the scripted stepchild. From the beginnings, a distinct breed of entrepreneurs and hucksters made their way to the city's Lake Michigan shores seeking oportunity. No amount of tragedy could persuade them from their enterprises, be they legal or not. Two days after the Great Chicago Fire of 1871 had reduced most of the city to ashes, one real-estate broker posted a sign reading: "All gone but wife, children and energy."

Afterward, the city shucked its 19th-century past and became the most modern metropolis in the country, if not the world, home to the first skyscraper and a new Prairie School of architecture in sync with the low, limitless horizon of the region. Musicians came and amped up the blues. Gangsters grabbed a piece of the action and held on. Everyone thought big. "Make no little plans," said former Chicago city planner and architect Daniel Burnham, "they have no magic to stir men's blood."

The spirit of optimism that marks the commercial aspects of the city is distinct on a personal level too. It's a common stereotype that Midwesterners are friendly; Chicagoans are often that and much more—honest, opinionated and curious. It takes optimism to emigrate and Chicago received wave after wave of Scandinavians and Germans early on, and still welcomes incoming Irish, Polish, Mexicans and Filipinos.

Chicago is perhaps the most American city of all.

Facts + Figures

- Residents: 2.8 million
- Companies: 354,751
- Tourists: 30 million per year
- Ranking: 7th most expensive city in the US
- Visitors to the Navy Pier: 8 million per year

MUSICAL CHICAGO

Jazz has thrived in the city since the 1920s when New Orleans' innovators moved north. Louis Armstrong struck out on his own with the "Hot Five" recordings he made in town. Later, African-Americans moving up from the rural South settled in and took the traditional blues music electric. Both jazz and blues clubs still entertain today.

EDIBLE CHICAGO

In the early 20th century Chicago was a meat-and-potatoes town, home of stock-yards and slaughterhouses and the rail-road hub transporting beef to the outer regions. Steak houses, deep-dish pizza and hot dogs continue the tradition of substantive eating in Chicago. But in the past 25 years the city has nurtured a mod-ern band of chefs to become one of the most innovative places to eat in the US.

DESIGN CHICAGO

Architects and entrepreneurs engineered Chicago's phoenix after the Great Fire, inventing the skyscraper in the rebuilding. Daniel Burnham had bold plans for Chicago's front yard of parks that buffer city and shore. Frank Lloyd Wright found-ed his Prairie School of design here. Later innovators such as Mies van der Rohe also left their marks and bolstered Chicago's reputation as a great architecture town.

A Short Stay in Chicago

DAY 1

Morning Start your stay with a 9am stroll around **Millennium Park** (▷ 50) downtown, to walk across Frank Gehry's bridge and ogle the reflections on the highly polished bean-shaped sculpture by Anish Kapoor.

Mid-morning Walk the two blocks over to the **Art Institute of Chicago** (▷ 44). Doors open at 10.30 most days, 10 on weekends, and lines form at least 15 minutes prior. It's worth the effort to have the Impressionist galleries briefly to yourself.

Lunch Take a break and soak in the Loop atmosphere at **Atwood Café** (▷ 37), just a few blocks west of the museum on Washington and State streets.

Afternoon Head to Wabash and Washington where you can catch the elevated train, aka the **El** (▷ 26). Take the Brown Line bound for Kimball. Get off at the Belmont stop and walk to the opposite platform to catch the train heading back to the Loop.

Mid-afternoon Take a walk around the **Loop** to admire some public sculpture installed there (▷ 25). Start with the unnamed Picasso in Daley Center Plaza then go to the Calder at the Federal Center Plaza and the Jean Dubuffet at the James R. Thompson Center.

Dinner Reserve a table at Gibson's Steakhouse for the classic Chicago meal—big, beefy and boisterous.

Evening Get tickets to **Second City** (▷ 67) for a good guffaw over Chicago-style humor, which is topical and mostly improvised.

DAY 2

Morning Hop the 9.30 **Architecture River Cruise** (▷ 24) offered by the Chicago Architecture Foundation. The tours are a big draw and usually sell out so plan ahead and reserve before coming to town.

Mid-morning Disembark the boat and walk up the **Magnificent Mile** (▷ 68), the stretch of Michigan Avenue that runs from the Chicago River up to Oak Street, to check out the tony shopping district and a number of architectural landmarks including the **Wrigley Building** (▷ 72), **Tribune Tower** (▷ 72) and the John Hancock Building.

Lunch Stop for lunch at the **Museum of Contemporary Art** (▷ 71) where the celebrated Austrian-turned-Californian chef Wolfgang Puck runs a café in a sunny, art-filled space.

Afternoon Rent bikes at **Navy Pier** (▷ 64) and take a spin on the Lake Michigan shoreline past the popular **Oak Street** (▷ 71) and **North Avenue** (▷ 66) beaches to appreciate how Chicagoans play.

Mid-afternoon Ascend the **John Hancock Building** (▷ 60) and stop at the Signature Lounge on the 96th floor for drinks and the best view in town.

Dinner Sit down to order a sampling of wine perfectly paired to entrees as well as small, shareable plates at the innovative wine bar and café **Bin 36** (▷ 79).

Evening Take a cab to **Buddy Guy's Legends** (▷ 93) on the near South Side to catch a few sets of the blues before calling it a night.

Top 25

These pages are a quick guide to the Top 25, which are described in more detail later. Here they are listed alphabetically and the tinted background shows the area they are in.

Graceland Cemetery, Wrigley Field Stadium

Diversey Harbor

NORTH SIDE 55–80

Lincoln Park Zoo

Oz Park

Lincoln Park

North Avenue Beach

Lake Michigan

Wicker Park Boutique Browsing

Second City Theatre

OLD TOWN

Gold Coast

Stanton-Schiller Park

North Branch of Chicago River

Seward Park

Oak Street Beach

Frank Lloyd Wright Home and Studio

Washington Square

Gallery Hopping

NEAR NORTH

Hancock Center

Seneca Park

Lake Shore Park

Magnificent Mile

Outer Harbor

Milton Lee Olive Park

Navy Pier

Chicago River

Chicago Architecture Foundation River Cruise

THE LOOP 21–38

LOOP

Loop Sculpture

Millenium Park

SOUTH SIDE 81–94

El Train

Sears Tower

The Rookery

Butler Field

Art Institute of Chicago

Chicago Harbor

Biking on the Chicago Lakefront

Sheridan Park

Grant Park

John G Shedd Aquarium

Adler Planetarium and Astronomy Museum

Standiford Park

Field Museum of Natural History

MUSEUM CAMPUS 39–54

SOUTH LOOP

Burnham Park Harbor

Northerly Island

Dvorak Park

CHINATOWN

Prairie Avenue Historic District

Burnham Park

South Branch of Chicago River

Du Sable Museum of African American History

Museum of Science and Industry

ESSENTIAL CHICAGO TOP 25

9

Shopping

Chicago's shops can excite the purchasing passions of the entire Midwest while surprising and delighting visitors from much farther afield. The upscale malls and boutiques on and around the Magnificent Mile attest to the international nature of the city, while the plethora of smaller independent outlets show that the city has retained its own character against the onslaught of globalized retailing.

Shopping Streets

For designer clothing, the Magnificent Mile is the showplace of Chicago. Men and women in pursuit of quality attire will find most major names represented in the high-rise malls along Michigan Avenue. For those who like a more personal shopping experience, a stroll around nearby Oak Street finds a clutch of elegant boutiques offering European haute couture and eager assistants. The same area hosts many of the city's major art galleries and antiques dealers.

Antiques and Retro

More fine art and antiques dealers can be found in River North, while their brasher, funkier counterparts are a feature in the shopping districts of Lake View and Wicker Park. There is also an abundance of outlets for extreme clothing, new and vintage, and bizarre household furnishings, often made by local craftspeople.

THE LOOP

Historic department stores such as Carson Pirie Scott and Marshall Field's, now a Macy's, are reminders of the glory days of the Loop, when it was the social hub of the city. This role was ended by the population and retail shift to suburbia and the Loop became solely a place of work, symbolized by its high-rise office towers. Aided by a 1990s rejuvenation that saw 1920s-style lampposts and subway entrances appear, the Loop has enjoyed a minor revival.

Souvenirs

Simple souvenirs can be found at the Magnificent Mile malls, but more choices at better prices can be found among the touristy shops of Navy Pier. Alternatives to miniatures of high-rise buildings, such as Sears Tower and Hancock Tower, and T-shirts, plates and fridge magnets bearing images of the skyline seen from Lake Michigan include the genuine municipal cast-offs, such as sewer covers and parking meters, offered by the Chicago Store on E. Pearson Street.

Tasty Reminders

Sausages might seem an unlikely reminder of Chicago but the city has been shaped by people of Eastern European descent, with the result that Polish (and that of other Eastern European nationalities) handmade sausages, with various meats, flavorings and spices, are a feature of many delis. For a quick bite, try the distinctive hot dogs and deep-dish pizza.

Books and Music

Surviving the rising tide of international chains, Chicago retains an impressive number of independent bookstores; 57th Street in Hyde Park holds several. Likewise, the city's strong jazz and blues pedigree is represented by specialist CD and vinyl outlets often featuring new Chicago-based musicians alongside established names.

ESSENTIAL CHICAGO SHOPPING

SPORTING SOUVENIRS

The city that produced basketball's Michael Jordan and made a celebrity of baseball's Sammy Sosa is unsurprisingly rich in sporting lore and offers mementoes and much memorabilia. Baseball's White Sox and Cubs both have outlets close to their stadiums, and that of the latter, the legendary Wrigley Field, has a souvenir industry all of its own. The merchandise of football's Chicago Bears and basketball's Chicago Bulls is also prevalent around the city.

Shopping by Theme

Whether you're looking for a department store, a quirky boutique or something inbetween, you'll find it all in Chicago. On this page shops are listed by theme. For a more detailed write-up, see the individual listings in Chicago by Area.

ACCESSORIES

The Alley (▷ 103)
Beatnix (▷ 103)
Belmont Army Surplus
  (▷ 103)
The Daisy Shop (▷ 74)
Stitch (▷ 99)

ART AND ANTIQUES

Broadway Antique Market
  (▷ 103)
Illinois Artisans Shop
  (▷ 33)
Pagoda Red (▷ 99)
Poster Plus (▷ 34)
P.O.S.H. (▷ 74)
R. H. Love Galleries
  (▷ 75)

BOOKS

57th Street Books
  (▷ 103)
After-Words (▷ 74)
Booksamillion (▷ 33)
Chicago Architecture
  Foundation (▷ 34)
Graham Crackers Comics
  (▷ 33)
Powell's Bookstore (▷ 33)
Prairie Avenue Bookshop
  (▷ 34)
Rand McNally (▷ 34)
Unabridged Bookstore
  (▷ 103)

CLOTHES AND SHOES

Banana Republic (▷ 74)
Barneys New York (▷ 74)
Brooks Bros (▷ 74)
City Soles (▷ 99)
Helen Yi (▷ 99)
J Crew (▷ 74)
Lord & Taylor (▷ 74)
Old Navy (▷ 33)
P45 (▷ 99)
Prada (▷ 75)
Scoop NYC (▷ 99)
Sugar Magnolia (▷ 75)
Ultimo (▷ 75)

DISCOUNT OUTLETS

H&M (▷ 33)
Nordstrom Rack (▷ 34)
DSW Shoe Warehouse
  (▷ 103)
T. J. Maxx (▷ 34)

HOME

Embelezar (▷ 99)

DEPT STORES AND MALLS

The Atrium Mall (▷ 33)
Carson Pirie Scott & Co
  Store (▷ 33)
Chicago Place (▷ 74)
The Jeweler's Center
  (▷ 33)
Marshall Field's (▷ 34)
Navy Pier (▷ 74)
Neiman-Marcus (▷ 74)
900 North Michigan
  (▷ 74)
Shops at the Mart (▷ 74)
Water Tower Place
  (▷ 74)
Westfield North Bridge
  (▷ 75)

MISCELLANEOUS

Blick Art Materials (▷ 33)
Chicago Music Mart
  (▷ 33)
The Savvy Traveler
  (▷ 34)
Sportsworld (▷ 103)
Tower Records (▷ 34)
Uncle Fun (▷ 103)

Chicago by Night

Sun Down
After the sun sets, much of the Magnificent Mile (▷ 68) and parts of the Loop are bathed in twinkling lights. The Wrigley Building (▷ 72) seen from Michigan Avenue Bridge is famously stunning, while the illuminated profile of the John Hancock Center (▷ 96) makes the towering building seem even taller. From it, or the Loop's Sears Tower (▷ 28–29), a night-time viewing reveals the grid-style patterns of city neighborhoods stretching into the distance and the blackness of Lake Michigan dotted by the lights of scattered ships.

Warm Nights
Warm nights during spring, summer and fall find Chicagoans outdoors, making the most of bars and restaurants with patio tables. With its hotels and late-opening shops, the Magnificent Mile is lively after dark, but there is more taking place in the nightlife strips of residential neighborhoods. The Gold Coast sections of Division, Oak and Elm streets are worth a look, as are the main drags of Wicker Park and Lake View. More commercially oriented nightlife is found amid the theme bars and clubs of River North.

Winter Wonders
Cold and snowy Chicago may sometimes be, but dull it never is. The winter period marks a high point of the cultural calendar with the classical concert, opera and ballet seasons fully into their stride, and a complete program of theater, rock and pop music.

CHICAGO BLUES
When the nationwide chain of House of Blues opened in the River North entertainment district in the 1990s, it marked a full circle for the city where South Side clubs gave birth to the urban electric blues. In such places, generally smaller and friendlier than the more tourist-oriented North Side venues, it can still be heard.

Eating Out

Meat and More

Chicago is a city of hearty appetites, guaranteeing you a good meal whether at the local hot dog stand or at one of the city's marquee restaurants. Headquarters to the nation's slaughterhouses in the 19th century, Chicago is famed for its steakhouses such as the classic Gene & Georgetti's and beef sandwich shops, including Al's Italian Beef. But in recent years it has emerged as a culinary leader on the fine dining front, with celebrated meals from top chefs Charlie Trotter (Charlie Trotter's) and Rick Bayless (Frontera Grill and Topolobampo) and next-generation culinary experimenter Grant Achatz (Alinea).

Ethnic Eats

Immigrant neighborhoods of Poles, Indians, Vietnamese, Chinese and Italians, among others, lay their tables richly with authentic homeland foods; visit Milwaukee Avenue for Polish borscht, Devon Street for Indian *dal*, Argyle Street for Vietnamese *pho* or Chinatown for dum sum. Tasty and often thrifty adventures with myriad dining choices line those streets.

Street Food

Chicago is perhaps best known for its street food, highlighted by Chicago-style hot dogs "dragged through the garden" (with vegetable toppings) and deep-dish pizza where a thick crust holds heaps of cheese, cured meats and vegetables—a meal in a single slice.

CHICAGO DEEP-DISH PIZZA

In Chicago the Mediterranean staple pizza got hefty when, in 1943, Pizzeria Uno founder Ike Sewell pulled up the crust in a deep pizza pan and heaped in toppings. The founders of the Lou Malnati's pizzeria chain worked in Sewell's kitchen at the time and claim a slice of the history too. Today Chicagoans still argue about who's got the best deep-dish with other culinary competitors including Gino's East.

Restaurants by Cuisine

There are restaurants to suit all tastes and budgets in Chicago. On this page they are listed by cuisine. For a more detailed description of each restaurant, see Chicago by Area.

If You Like...

However you'd like to spend your time in Chicago, these top
suggestions should help you tailor your ideal visit.
Each sight or listing has a fuller write-up in Chicago by Area.

CARTING THE KIDS

See the dolphin show at the Shedd Aquarium
(▷ 49).
Hit Navy Pier (▷ 64) for the Children's Museum
and Ferris wheel.
Make the acquantaince of T. rex Sue at the
Field Museum (▷ 46).
Visit the apes at the Lincoln Park Zoo (▷ 62).

OGLING THE ARCHITECTURE

Trek to Frank Lloyd Wright's Home & Studio
(▷ 100).
Take the Architecture River Cruise with the
Chicago Architecture Foundation (▷ 24).
Tour the Robie House (▷ 91).
Visit the Glessner House (▷ 87).

SAVING MONEY

Dine on Chicago hot dogs or
personal deep-dish pizzas.
Ride the El for a budget skyline tour
(▷ 26).
Go to the Lincoln Park Zoo (▷ 62);
it's free.
Catch a band outdoors at the Navy Pier
beer garden, also free (▷ 64).

SHOW GOING

Get tickets to the Goodman Theater
(▷ 36) in the Loop.
Spot the celebs on stage at the
Steppenwolf Theater (▷ 77).
Laugh it up at Second City (▷ 67).

DINING WITH A VIEW

Reserve a table at Everest (▷ 37) for western views.

Dine amid the skyline at the Signature Room on the 95th floor in the John Hancock Building (▷ 60).

Go to NoMI, which frames the Historic Water Tower (▷ 70) from its 7th-floor perch.

Regard the lake and Oak Street Beach from Spiaggia (▷ 80).

NIGHTCRAWLING

Hit the Green Mill Cocktail Lounge (▷ 104) for a live jazz set.

Get the blues at Buddy Guy's Legends (▷ 35).

Check out the local and touring acts on stage at the Metro (▷ 104).

Visit Stone Lotus (▷ 77) and soak up the scene.

SOUVENIR SHOPPING

Illinois Artisans Shop (▷ 33) for local artist-made crafts.

Navy Pier shops for trinkets, snowglobes and Chicago Police Department T-shirts (▷ 74).

City of Chicago Store for street signs and even parking meters.

Hit the Wrigley Field (▷ 59) region for Cubs paraphernalia.

FASHION WITH EDGE

Ultimo (▷ 75) for a mix of high-end designers.

City Soles (▷ 99) for funky shoes.

P45 (▷ 99) for emerging American designers.

GOING GREEN

Walk the art- and architecture-filled Millennium Park (▷ 50).
Get to Grant Park (▷ 51) in the evening for a look at Buckingham Fountain's light show.
Visit the greenhouses of the Garfield Park Conservatory (▷ 102).
Tour Lincoln Park , home to a zoo, conservatory, gardens and beaches (▷ 62, 71).

OUTWARD BOUND ACTION

Ride a bike along 18 miles (29km) of shoreline parkway (▷ 84).
Get in on a game of sand volleyball at the North Avenue Beach (▷ 66).
Swim with the triathletes in Lake Michigan.

LOCAL FOOD

Have a dog "dragged through the garden" at Gold Coast Dogs (▷ 79).
Line up for a high-fat breakfast at Lou Mitchell's (▷ 38).
Devour a slice or two of deep-dish pizza at Lou Malnati's or Chicago's Pizzeria Uno (▷ 80).
Try an Italian beef sandwich from Mr. Beef.

HAUT HOTELS

Have high tea at the Ritz-Carlton Chicago (▷ 112).
Be pampered at the spa in the Peninsula hotel (▷ 112).
Join the swells for Sunday brunch at the Four Seasons (▷ 112).
Ogle the multimillion dollar art collection at the Park Hyatt Chicago (▷ 112).

Chicago by Area

THE LOOP

MUSEUM CAMPUS

NORTH SIDE

SOUTH SIDE

FARTHER AFIELD

The Loop

Named for the elevated train that rings the district, the downtown Loop is where Chicago does business. The historic center is also the seat of government and the oldest shopping district in the city.

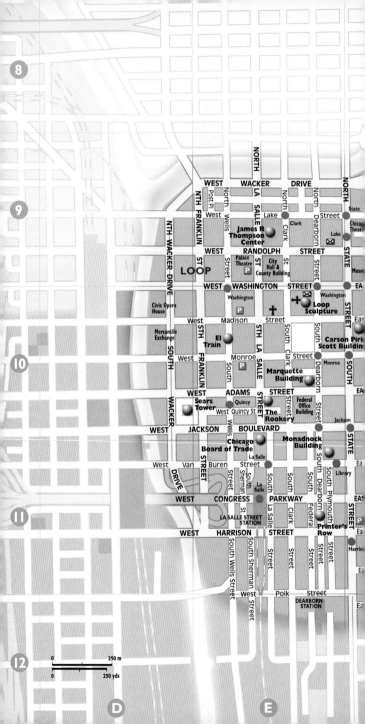

Chicago Architecture
Foundation River Cruise

Chicago

WACKER DRIVE

EAST

NORTH

Athenaeum

South

North
Michigan

Water Street

North
Stetson
Avenue

East Garland

Illinois
Center

East
Wabash

Randolph

Lake Street

Prudential
Building

Michigan Avenue

EAST RANDOLPH DRIVE

Randolph
Court

Chicago
Cultural
Center

RANDOLPH
STREET
STATION

ASHINGTON
STREET

Madison

Chicago
Athenaeum

Madison St

South

South
Michigan

Lake

Michigan

Adams
ADAMS ST

South
Wabash

Michigan Avenue

Orchestra
Hall

🛈

Michigan Avenue

an Buren St

Congress Plaza

South
Wabash

ONGRESS
ARKWAY

Americana
Congress

Chicago
Harbor

rrison Street

Museum of
Contemporary
Photography

Blackstone
Theatre

albo Avenue

East Balbo Drive

Spertus Museum
of Judaica

th Street

th
Avenue

F

G

Chicago Architecture Foundation River Cruise

Chicago cruise boats

THE BASICS

www.architecture.org

➕ F9

✉ 224 Michigan Avenue (board at dock location at Michigan Avenue and Wacker Drive)

☎ 312/922-3432

🕐 10 sailings daily in summer. Closed Dec–Apr

🚇 El stop: Brown Line: Randolph

🚌 144, 146, 151

♿ Expensive

HIGHLIGHTS

● Wrigley Building
● Marina Towers
● 333 W. Wacker Drive
● Chicago River bridges
● Sears Tower
● Tribune Tower

The best of the boat cruises that ply the Chicago River, the Chicago Architecture Foundation's river tours provide knowledgeable narration of 50 distinctive buildings in popular 90-minute outings.

Architectural historians Founded by architects and preservationists in 1966 to preserve the Glessner House on Prairie Avenue, the Chicago Architecture Foundation has grown into the city's most respected leader of design-oriented tours. Arresting buildings loom over passengers at water level gliding by at their bases. Volunteer docents (guides) narrate the trip covering Bertrand Goldberg's 1964 corn-cob-shape Marina City Towers, the triangular, white, tile-clad Wrigley Building erected by the chewing-gum magnate William Wrigley Jr., the black granite art deco tower of the Carbide & Carbon Building from the sons of city planner Daniel Burnham and the 1922-erected Tribune Building that, crowned by a series of Gothic flying buttresses inspired by a French cathedral, looks much older.

Chicago River In the 17th century Native Americans occupied the banks of the Chicago River where it met Lake Michigan. Over the next few centuries as the population grew, wastewater from the river flowed into Lake Michigan, contaminating the city's drinking water. So in 1900 engineers reversed the river's flow away from the lake and into the then-new Sanitary and Ship Canal.

The Flamingo *(below);* Monument with Standing Beast *(right)*

Loop Public Sculpture

A few blocks in Chicago's Loop district comprise an outdoor exhibition space devoted to some of the world's finest sculptors for those looking for a cultural self-guided walking tour.

The Collection In 1967 then-mayor Richard J. Daley dedicated the monumental, untitled sculpture by Pablo Picasso at Daley Center Plaza (Dearborn and Washington streets), considered the first noncommemorative city sculpture and the start of Chicago's strong public arts program highlighted by its collection in the Loop. Across Washington Street Joan Miró's depiction of a woman with outstretched arms faces the Picasso. Marc Chagall's stone mosaic *The Four Seasons* is at Dearborn and Monroe streets. Two blocks down at Dearborn and Adams, Alexander Calder's graceful, neon orange *Flamingo* contrasts with the dark glass Federal Center. Jean Dubuffet's white fiberglass *Monument with Standing Beast* resides at the James R. Thompson Center where Clark meets Randolph Street. And just over the Chicago River in the West Loop at 600 W. Madison Claes Oldenburg created *Batcolumn*, a 100-foot (328m) steel baseball bat.

Chicago's Picasso Chicago architect William Hartman convinced Pablo Picasso to create a sculpture for the city's Civic Center Plaza. Picasso's untitled work, "a gift to the people of Chicago," is today part of everyday Loop life, and skateboarders launch from its sloping base.

THE BASICS

www.cityofchicago.org/publicart

➕ E10

🚇 Brown, Red, Green Loop stops

🚌 20, 22

HIGHLIGHTS

● *Untitled* by Pablo Picasso
● *Flamingo* by Alexander Calder
● *Monument with Standing Beast* by Jean Dubuffet
● *Chicago* by Joan Miró
● *Batcolumn* by Claus Oldenburg
● *The Four Seasons* by Marc Chagall

Riding the El Train

TOP 25

The El Train crossing the Chicago River (left); Quincy station (below)

THE BASICS

www.transitchicago.com

🔲 E10

☎ 888/968-7282

🕐 Mon–Fri 5am–midnight, Sat–Sun 7am–midnight

🚉 El stop: Brown Line Loop stops

🚌 29

💲 Inexpensive

HIGHLIGHTS

● Crossing the Chicago River aboard the Brown Line
● Seeing into baseball's Wrigley Field from the Addison stop on the Red Line
● Snaking around the downtown high-rises aboard the Brown Line

FACTS

● Blue Line, largely underground, efficiently connects O'Hare airport to downtown
● The elevated Orange Line links Midway Airport and downtown

One of Chicago's most distinctive symbols, the elevated train, El or L for short, provides a commuter's close-up of the city's downtown district as well as its neighborhood backyards.

Tracking history New York erected the first elevated train in 1867, a feat Chicago soon copied in a flurry of companies devoted to the project. The first line (3.6 miles/5.8km), opened in 1892, was nicknamed the "Alley L" for running above city-owned alleys, sparing the transit company from securing access privileges from the property owners. Expansion of the El lines was linked to many major events in Chicago history including the World's Columbian Exhibition and the need to get workers to the Stock Yards. Independently owned rail lines agreed to link their services downtown in a "Union Loop" in 1897, the origin of the district's name. Chicago Transit Authority today operates seven color-coded routes over 222 miles (357km) of track.

Brown Line The best line for sightseers, the Brown Line rings the downtown Loop, crosses the Chicago River heading north through the neighborhoods of River North, Lincoln Park, Lakeview and Lincoln Square before terminating at Kimball Street. Board anywhere in the Loop to enjoy weaving through the high-rises two stories up from street level. Disembark anywhere on the route and, using overhead platform bridges that connect north-and southbound tracks without a transit fee, return in the opposite direction.

Interior of The Rookery building (below); detail of the exterior of the building (right)

The Rookery

Designed by Daniel Burnham and John Wellborn Root in the 1880s, and later renovated by Frank Lloyd Wright, the Rookery is among Chicago's most admired landmarks.

Birdhouse After the Great Fire of 1871, birds took to roosting in the water-storage building that was temporarily City Hall. It was consequently nicknamed the Rookery. Public feeling dictated that the building that replaced it should formally take on this name. Rising 11 floors, the Rookery was among the tallest buildings in the world on completion and one of the most important early skyscrapers: The thick load-bearing brick-and-granite walls at the base, decorated with Roman, Moorish and Venetian (and several rook) motifs, support upper levels with an iron frame that enabled the structure to be raised higher than previously thought possible. With its masonry exterior and iron interior, the Rookery is considered by architectural historians to be a transitional building in the evolution of the modern skyscraper.

Interior treasures The facade, however, is scant preparation for the interior. The inner court is bathed in incredible levels of natural light entering through a vast domed skylight. Imposing lamps hang above the floor, and Root's intricate ironwork decorates the stairways that climb up to a 360-degree balcony. The white marble, introduced by Frank Lloyd Wright in 1905, increases the sense of space and brightness

THE BASICS

+ E10
- ✉ 209 S. La Salle Street
- ☎ 312/553-6150
- 🕐 Lobby open during business hours
- 🚇 Brown and Orange Lines: Quincy
- 🚌 1, 22, 60, 151
- ♿ Good
- 🎫 Free

HIGHLIGHTS

- Light-flooded, glass-roofed inner court
- Ten-story spiral staircase
- Prairie-style light fixtures
- External terra-cotta ornamentation
- Carrara marble walls
- Mosaic tile floors

THE LOOP

★

TOP 25

Sears Tower

- Visibility of up to 50 miles (80km)
- Views to four states on a clear day
- Feeling the building sway
- High-powered telescopes
- Sunset views after 4pm
- Terminals with tower information in six languages

FACTS

- Six robotic window washers mounted on the roof clean all the 16,000 windows
- Elevators soar 1,600 feet (487m) per minute

Although it is no longer the world's tallest building, the Sears Tower rises higher than any other structure in the city. As well as unique and stylish architecture, it has the highest man-made vantage point in the western hemisphere.

Built from tubes From 1974 to 1996, the Sears Tower's 110 floors and 1,454ft (443m) height made it the tallest building in the world, rising from the Loop with a distinctive profile of black aluminum and bronze-tinted glass. Architect Bruce Graham, of Skidmore, Owings & Merrill, structured it around nine 75sq ft (7sq m) bundled tubes, which decline in number as the building reaches upward. Aside from increasing the colossal structure's strength, this technique also echoes the stepback, New York skyscraper style of the late

Clockwise from top left: People on the observation deck of the Sears Tower; the Chicago skyline seen from Sears Tower; looking down to the Chicago River from the tower; detail of the main entrance

1920s. Among the early tasks during the three-year construction was the creation of foundation supports capable of holding a 222,500-ton building. The two rooftop antennae were added in 1982, increasing the building's height by 253ft (77m) and serving the many broadcasting organizations based inside the tower.

Seeing for miles Although the audiovisual presentation on Chicago at street level is uninspiring, the 103rd-floor Skydeck is not. Accessible via a 70-second elevator ride, it reveals a panorama of the city and its surroundings. A recorded commentary describes the view and landmark buildings. Sears, the retail company that commissioned the building and used its lower floors, moved out in 1992. Note Alexander Calder's moving sculpture, *Universe*, in the lobby.

THE BASICS

www.thesearstower.com
🚩 D10
✉ 233 S. Wacker Drive
☎ 312/875-9696
🕐 Skydeck: May–Sep daily 10–10; Oct–Apr daily 10–8. May be closed in high winds
🍽 Various restaurants and cafés
🚇 Brown and Orange Lines: Quincy
🚌 1, 60, 151, 156
♿ Excellent
💲 Moderate

29

More to See

CARSON PIRIE SCOTT & COMPANY BUILDING

The elaborately decorated exterior was created by Louis Sullivan over a five-year period beginning in 1899. The more austere terra-cotta-clad upper levels express the steel form of the building. The large windows span the entire width between the steel supports: known as "Chicago windows," they accentuate the horizontal, maximize the amount of natural light reaching the interior and strengthen the general sense of geometric cohesion. A 1979 renovation restored many of Sullivan's features.

✚ F10 ✉ 1 S. State Street ☎ 312/641-7000 🕐 Tue–Wed, Fri–Sat 9.45–5.45, Mon and Thu 9.45–7.30 🚇 Blue line: Madison. Red Line: Monroe 🚌 22, 23, 36, 56, 157 ♿ Good 🎫 Free

CHICAGO CULTURAL CENTER

The Washington Street entrance leads visitors through hefty bronze doors set beneath a Romanesque portal into the main lobby, whose grand staircase is bordered by exquisite mosaics set into its white Carrara marble balustrades. A visitor information office occupies part of the next floor, as does the hall and rotunda of the Great Army of the Republic, another exhibition space, with Tennessee marble walls and mosaic tile floor, while the floor above holds the Preston Bradley Hall, with an awe-inspiring Tiffany-glass dome. The main exhibition hall is on the top level, where decorated columns rise to meet an immaculately coffered ceiling.

✚ F9 ✉ 78 E. Washington Street ☎ 312/629-6630 🕐 Mon–Thu 10–7, Fri 10–5, Sat 10–5, Sun 11–5 🍽 Café 🚇 Brown and Orange Lines: Madison 🚌 3, 4, 60, 145, 147, 151

JAMES R. THOMPSON CENTER (1985)

This glass-and-steel edifice includes a soaring atrium lined with stores, restaurants and cafés; upper levels house state agencies.

✚ E9 ✉ 100 W. Randolph Street ☎ 312/814-6684 🚇 Blue, Brown and Orange Lines: Clark/Lake 🚌 156 ♿ Good

Chicago Cultural Center (above)

Corner entrance to the Carson Pirie Scott & Company Building

MARQUETTE BUILDING

Completed in 1895, the Marquette Building is among the unsung masterpieces of Chicago architecture. It demonstrates the first use of the three-part "Chicago window"—plate glass spans the whole width between the building's steel supports. Lobby reliefs record the expedition of French Jesuit missionary Jacques Marquette; the entrance doors' panther heads are by Edward Kemeys, also responsible for the lions fronting the Art Institute of Chicago (▷ 44).

✚ E10 ✉ 140 S. Dearborn Street
🚇 Brown and Orange Lines: Quincy

MUSEUM OF CONTEMPORARY PHOTOGRAPHY

In addition to the museum's collection of American photography, you will find varied temporary exhibitions of contemporary photography from around the world.

✚ F11 ✉ 600 S. Michigan Avenue
☎ 312/344-7104 🕐 Mon–Fri 10–5, Sat noon–5 🚇 Red Line: Harrison 🚌 1, 3, 4, 6, 38, 146 ♿ Good 💲 Free

PRINTER'S ROW

The industrial buildings lining Dearborn Street were the core of Chicago's printing industry during the late 19th century. Many are now loft-style apartments, with galleries and restaurants.

✚ E11 ✉ Dearborn Street 🚇 Blue line: La Salle; Red Line: Harrison 🚌 22, 62

SPERTUS MUSEUM OF JUDAICA

Torah scrolls, Hanukkah lamps and tools used in circumcision are among the decorative and religious objects spanning 5,000 years that form the core of this museum's extensive collection of Judaica. However, only a small selection can be shown at any time. The richness of most exhibits contrasts strongly with the somber collection of Holocaust memorabilia.

✚ F11 ✉ 618 S. Michigan Avenue
☎ 312/322-1747 🕐 Sun–Wed 10–5, Thu 10–7, Fri 10–3 🚇 Red Line: Harrison 🚌 1, 3, 4, 6, 38, 146 ♿ Good 💲 Inexpensive; free Fri

Inside the Museum of Contemporary Photography (above)

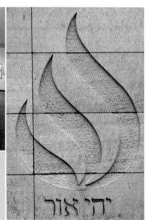

Engravings on the exterior of the Spertus Museum of Judaica (right)

Loop the Loop

The best way to see the many architectural and artistic highlights of the Loop is to walk from point to point.

DISTANCE: 2 miles (3km) **ALLOW:** 60–90 minutes

START

SEARS TOWER (▷ 28)
🚇 Brown, Orange Lines: Quincy

END

CHICAGO CULTURAL CENTER (▷ 30)
🚇 Brown, Orange Lines: Madison

1 Begin at Sears Tower (1974), until 1996 the world's tallest building, with a fantastic view from its 103rd-floor Skydeck.

8 End by strolling north along Michigan Avenue to the Chicago Cultural Center (1897), at the junction with Washington Street.

2 Continue along Jackson Boulevard for the Chicago Board of Trade (1930), observing the trading from the visitors' gallery.

7 Continue to Louis Sullivan's early 20th-century Carson Pirie Scott & Co Building. Walk west on Madison to Dearborn, then one block south for the Marquette Building (1895).

3 Turn north along La Salle Street and peek inside the architecturally stunning Rookery. Continue north to the junction with Randolph Street.

6 Take a closer look at Miró's sculpture, *Chicago*, marking the plaza of 69 W. Washington Street. Stroll south along the bustling State Street, passing the glass and terra-cotta Reliance Building.

4 Turn east on Washington to look inside the Richard J. Daley Center. Leave by the Washington Street side to view the 50ft-tall (15m) untitled Picasso sculpture.

5 Continue east down Washington to State Street.

WALK

THE LOOP

Shopping

THE ATRIUM MALL
Diverse stores provide an excellent excuse to stroll around the spectacular second floor of this dazzling atrium, a pastiche of glass, marble and steel, with an impressive waterfall.
E9 ✉ James R. Thompson Center, 100 W. Randolph Street ☎ 312/346-0777 Blue, Brown, Orange Lines: Clark/Lake 🚌 156

BLICK ART MATERIALS
Art supply store Blick stocks everything from oil paints to sculptor's clay. Sketchpads and kids' projects appeal to travelers.
F10 ✉ 36 S. State Street ☎ 312/920-0300 Red Line: Madison 🚌 29

BOOKSAMILLION
There could well be a million books, mostly mainstream titles on diverse subjects, amid these tightly stacked shelves.
E10 ✉ 144 S. Clark Street ☎ 312/857-0613 Blue and Red Lines: Washington 🚌 22, 24

CARSON PIRIE SCOTT & CO STORE
Though better known for its exterior architecture (▷ 30), the store has provided middle-class Chicagoans with good clothing, cosmetics and household accessories for years.
F10 ✉ 1 S. State Street

☎ 312/641-7000 Blue Line: Madison; Red Line: Monroe 🚌 22, 23, 36, 56, 157

CHICAGO ARCHITECTURE FOUNDATION
Exemplary source of books on architecture.
F11 ✉ 224 S. Michigan Avenue ☎ 312/922-3432 Brown, Orange Lines: Adams 🚌 3, 4, 6, 38

CHICAGO MUSIC MART
Pianos, ocarinas and Indian tablas are among the instruments you can find at this gathering of music retailers. Or look for the musically themed sweets.
F11 ✉ 333 S. State Street ☎ 312/362-6700 Blue, Red Lines: Jackson 🚌 1, 7, 60, 126, 145, 146, 147, 151

GRAHAM CRACKERS COMICS
This well-stocked comic-book store appeals to the

area's college students and serial aficionados.
F10 ✉ 77 E. Madison Street ☎ 312/620-1810 Red Line: Madison 🚌 29

H&M
Swedish designer knock-off shop, with featured lines by some actual designers including Stella McCartney, sells cheap and chic women's clothing.
F9 ✉ 24 N. State Street ☎ 312/263-4436 Red Line: Washington 🚌 29

ILLINOIS ARTISANS SHOP
On the second floor of the James R. Thompson Center, Illinois Artisans Shop showcases the work of artists around the state working in jewelry, ceramics, wood and textiles with semi-annual exhibits of fine art, including painting, photography, printmaking, drawing and sculpture.
E9 ✉ James R. Thompson Center, 100 W. Randolph Street ☎ 312/814-5321 Blue, Brown, Orange Lines: Clark/Lake 🚌 156

THE JEWELER'S CENTER
Jewelry and related products are sold in more than 140 outlets on 13 floors; if you can't find what you're looking for here, you never will.
F10 ✉ 5 S. Wabash Avenue ☎ 312/853-2057 Brown, Orange Lines: Madison 🚌 38

PRINTER'S ROW BOOK FAIR
To celebrate the district's history in print production the annual Printer's Row Book Fair held over a weekend in early June lures 150 new, used and antiques booksellers to temporary shops under tents lining South Dearborn between Congress and Taylor. Event programs include author readings and signings, and discussions.

THE LOOP

SHOPPING

MARSHALL FIELD'S

Chicagoans adore this department store, which carries clothing, household goods, jewelry, exotic foods, books and more. There are several branches in Chicago, but this is the best. The building has a Tiffany-glass dome, and the interior design outdoes Carson Pirie Scott and adds glamour. The store's own Frango Mints, sold in the basement Market Place section, make a good Chicagoan souvenir.

F10 111 N. State Street 312/781-1000 Blue, Red Lines: Washington 6, 11, 29, 36, 44, 62, 146

NORDSTROM RACK

www.nordstrom.com

The Rack takes up to 70 percent off full-price goods sold at sibling retailer Nordstrom, a Seattle-based department store best known for its quality clothing and shoe selection.

F10 24 N. State Street 312/377-5500 Red Line: Washington 29

OLD NAVY

www.oldnavy.com

A lower cost spin-off from the popular casual clothier Gap, Old Navy dresses infants to seniors in inexpensive, on-trend styles that make no pretense to endure more than a season. Shop to a disco soundtrack on two levels.

F10 35 N. State Street

312/551-0522 Red Line: Washington 29

POSTER PLUS

Historic posters, mostly celebrating landmarks in Chicago and US history, though many are attractive reprints rather than originals.

F11 200 S. Michigan Avenue 800/659-1905 Brown, Orange Lines: Adams 3, 4, 6, 38

POWELL'S BOOKSTORE

www.powellschicago.com

New, used and discount bookstore primarily serving local universities with a strong collection of classics.

F12 828 S. Wabash Avenue 312/341-0748 Red Line: Harrison 129

PRAIRIE AVENUE BOOKSHOP

Beloved independent

bookstore that caters to design fans with 20,000 architecture-related books in cluttered but cozy confines that encourage browsing.

F11 418 S. Wabash Avenue 800/474-2724 Blue, Red Lines: Jackson 29, 126

THE SAVVY TRAVELER

Everything travelers might need—from money belts to guidebooks.

F11 310 S. Michigan Avenue 312/913-9800 Brown, Orange Lines: Adams 3, 4, 6, 38

T. J. MAXX

www.tjmaxx.com

Another discount clothing chain; this one assembles mid-market looks for women.

F9 11 N. State Street 312/553-0515 Red Line: Washington 29

TOWER RECORDS

Three floors of music and movies aptly located behind Symphony Center.

F11 214 S. Wabash Avenue 312/663-0660 Brown Line: Adams 29

Entertainment and Nightlife

AUDITORIUM THEATER

www.auditoriumtheater.org
Designed by the revered Adler & Sullivan, the marvelously renovated Auditorium Building was the world's heaviest structure when completed in 1889. Excellent acoustics and good sightlines make it a fine venue for dance, music and drama productions.

➕ F11 ✉ 50 E. Congress Parkway ☎ 312/922-2110 🚇 Red Line: Harrison 🚌 6, 145, 146, 147, 151

BASE BAR

www.basebarchicago.com
The trendy lobby bar in the Hard Rock Hotel rocks out via a mini-stage that hosts live impromptu shows, sometimes by major stars, and TVs showing music videos.

➕ F9 ✉ 230 N. Michigan Avenue ☎ 312/345-1000 🚇 Red Line: Lake 🚌 143, 144, 145, 146

BIG BAR

www.hyatt.com
Size is everything at this boisterous bar in the Hyatt Regency Chicago, credited with making the world's largest margarita, in a cement mixer.

➕ F9 ✉ 151 E. Wacker Drive ☎ 312/565-1234 🚇 Red Line: Lake 🚌 1143, 144, 145, 146

BUDDY GUY'S LEGENDS

www.buddyguys.com
Co-owner and famed blues guitarist Buddy Guy presents outstanding blues acts, including internationally known names and local rising stars.

➕ F11 ✉ 754 S. Wabash Avenue ☎ 312/427-0333 🚇 Red Line: Harrison 🚌 12

CADILLAC PALACE THEATRE

One of the major theaters along Randolph Street comprising the Loop's theater district, the Cadillac Palace is often booked by big Broadway touring companies.

➕ E9 ✉ 151 W. Randolph Street ☎ 312/977-1700 🚇 Brown, Orange Lines: Washington 🚌 156

CHASE AUDITORIUM

www.npr.org
The satirical National Public Radio news-quiz show "Wait, Wait…Don't Tell me!" tapes its shows live each Thursday night

---

COMEDY SHOWS

Two comedy shows have been entertaining Chicago theatergoers for years. *Tony 'n' Tina's Wedding* (✉ 230 W. North Avenue ☎ 312/664-8844) re-creates an Italian-American wedding; the performers mingle with the audience ("the guests"). Meanwhile, *Late Nite Catechism* (✉ Royal George Theater, 1641 N. Halsted ☎ 312/988-9000) is a one-woman-show on Wednesday, Friday, Saturday and Sunday.

---

in this bank building basement auditorium.

➕ E10 ✉ 10 S. Dearborn Street ☎ 888/924-8924 🚇 Red Line: Monroe 🚌 29

CHICAGO THEATRE

www.thechicagotheatre.com
The 3,600-seat, French baroque-style Chicago Theatre with the classic vertical C-H-I-C-A-G-O spelled out on the marquee hosts concert tours in rock, jazz, hip-hop and ballet, as well as limited-run theater productions.

➕ F9 ✉ 175 N. State Street ☎ 312/462-6363 🚇 Red Line: Lake 🚌 29

CIVIC OPERA HOUSE

www.civicoperahouse.com
The fine Lyric Opera of Chicago company performs from mid-September to early February at this art deco auditorium (which is also one of the main dance venues). Seats are sometimes available at the box office on the day of performance.

➕ D10 ✉ 20 N. Wacker Drive ☎ 312/419-0033 🚇 Brown, Orange Lines: Madison/Wells 🚌 129

ENCORE LIQUID LOUNGE

www.encorechicago.com
Run by the adjacent Hotel Allegro, next to the Cadillac Palace Theatre, Encore is a popular spot to gather for drinks before or after the curtain. A substantial list of small-plate appetizers such as

chili-orange duck quesadillas with mango salsa complements the cocktails.
⊕ E9 ✉ 171 W. Randolph Street ☎ 312/338-3788 Ⓜ Brown Line: Washington 🚌 156

FORD CENTER FOR THE PERFORMING ARTS/ ORIENTAL THEATER
Still called the Oriental by locals, this ornate, 2,180-seat theater reopened in 1998 after a painstaking restoration. The North Loop theater presents first-rate shows in its top-notch performance space.
⊕ E9 ✉ 24 W. Randolph Street ☎ 312/902-1400 Ⓜ Red, Brown, Green, Orange Lines: Lake 🚌 156

GENE SISKEL FILM CENTER
www.siskelfilmcenter.org
The School of the Arts Institute of Chicago runs this ambitious cinema named for a former, highly influential film critic. Two screens show independent, foreign and vintage films in repertory, the type of arty fare you won't find at the Cineplex.
⊕ F9 ✉ 164 N. State Street ☎ 312/846-2600 Ⓜ Red Line: Lake 🚌 29

GOODMAN THEATRE
www.goodman-theatre.org
The Goodman hosts some of the best drama in the city, including both

classics and cutting-edge contemporary productions. Well-known actors including Brian Dehenny and Marcia Gay Harden have performed here and, before they died, and playwrights August Wilson and Arthur Miller debuted plays here.
⊕ E9 ✉ 170 N. Dearborn Street ☎ 312/443-3800 Ⓜ Red Line: Washington 🚌 22, 24, 36, 62

HOT HOUSE
www.hothouse.net
Trendy, warehouse-like spot in the South Loop area, with eclectic music and an arty crowd.
⊕ G11 ✉ 31 W. Balbo Drive ☎ 312/362-9707 Ⓜ Red Line: Harrison 🚌 6, 146

THE LIVING ROOM
www.whotels.com
The style-focused W. Chicago City Center makes a lounge of its historic lobby, installing a

HALF-PRICE TICKETS
Hot Tix (✉ 72 E. Randolph Street or Water Works Visitor Center, 163 E. Pearson Street) offers half-price tickets for many of the day's theater events. A recorded message (☎ 312/977-1755) and website (www.hottix.org) lists the day's performances. Full-price advance tickets are also available from Hot Tix, as well as from Ticketmaster (☎ 312/559-1212).

DJ on the mezzanine who pumps the vibe to cocktailers arrayed on sofas.
⊕ E10 ✉ 172 W. Adams Street ☎ 312/332-1200 Ⓜ Brown Line: Quincy 🚌 156

SHUBERT THEATER
Dating back to the 19th century, the handsome Shubert is a rare reminder that theater once thrived in the Loop. Dance companies perform here, though it is not exclusively a dance theater. It is best known for its musicals.
⊕ F10 ✉ 22 W. Monroe Street ☎ 312/977-1701 Ⓜ Brown, Orange Lines: Madison/Wells

SYMPHONY CENTER
www.cso.org
From September to May the renowned Chicago Symphony Orchestra (CSO) is in residence in this sumptuous Greek Revival hall, built in 1904. Tickets are sold early, but some may be available on the day of performance. The Civic Orchestra of Chicago, a training orchestra that often gives free concerts, appears here and there is an annual jazz series.
⊕ F10 ✉ 220 S. Michigan Avenue ☎ 312/294-3000 Ⓜ Brown, Orange Lines: Adams 🚌 1, 3, 4, 6, 7, 38, 60

Restaurants

312 CHICAGO ($$$)

One of the best Italian specialists in the Loop, 312 Chicago adjoins the Allegro Hotel and like others near the theater district requires a reservation for a table prior to showtime.

➕ E9   ✉ 136 N. La Salle Street   ☎ 312/696-2420   🚇 Brown, Orange Lines: Washington   🚌 129

ATWOOD CAFÉ ($$)

Dine on hearty foods with an American accent such as maple-cured pork chops and chicken pot pie. Café staples such as salads and soups lighten up the lunch fare at this window-wrapped restaurant, which views the hustle and bustle of the Loop.

➕ E9   ✉ 1 W. Washington Street   ☎ 312/368-1900   🚇 Red Line: Washington   🚌 29

THE BERGHOFF CAFÉ ($$)

One of Chicago's oldest restaurants, the historic Berghoff serves classic German fare such as *sauerbraten* and *Weiner schnitzel* in an Old World-inspired room with stained-glass accents. The wood-panel upstairs bar makes a great stop for lunchtime sandwiches.

➕ E10   ✉ 17 W. Adams Street   ☎ 312/427-3170   🚇 Red Line: Jackson   🚌 29

CUSTOM HOUSE ($$$)

One of Chicago's most innovative chefs, Shawn McClain, gives the classic Chicago meat-centric menu an update with dishes such as veal cheeks and braised rabbit along with bone-in rib-eye steaks. Sleek and stylish interiors generate a clubby but unfussy vibe.

➕ E11   ✉ 500 S. Dearborn Street   ☎ 312/523-0200   🚇 Red Line: Harrison   🚌 129

EVEREST ($$$$)

This 40th-floor restaurant commanding spectacular views—beloved of financial wheeler-dealers—offers an updated and sometimes inspiring look at chef Jean Joho's native Alsace. The Loop location, prices and standards of cooking are all breathtakingly high.

➕ E10   ✉ 440 S. La Salle Street   ☎ 312/663-8920   🍽 Dinner only. Closed Sun, Mon   🚇 Blue Line: La Salle   🚌 22

HANNAH'S BRETZEL ($)

www.hannahsbretzel.com
Tiny Loop storefront sells unique German-style soft pretzels made with organic ingredients. Get them sliced, buttered, smeared with chocolate or filled with sandwich fixings. Grab and go; there are only a handful of seats in the store.

➕ E9   ✉ 180 W. Washington Street   ☎ 312/621-1111   🚇 Brown Line: Washington   🚌 156

HEAVEN ON SEVEN ($$)

This Cajun joint is tucked away on the seventh floor of a Loop office building, serving po' boy sandwiches, blackened fish and other spicy fare.

➕ F9   ✉ 111 N. Wabash Avenue   ☎ 312/263-6443   🚇 Red Line: Washington   🚌 29

THE ITALIAN VILLAGE RESTAURANTS ($$–$$$$)

Three Italians in one building, including the

DIM SUM

Served by many Chinese restaurants at lunchtime, dim sum is the term for small dishes wheeled around on trolleys. Stop a server who has dishes that look appetizing and take your pick. Popular dishes include *cha sil bow*—steamed pork bun; *gai bow*—steamed chicken bun; *chern goon*—spring rolls; and *sil mi*—steamed pork and shrimp dumpling. When you've eaten your fill, you will be charged by the plate.

expensive and smart Vivere, the mid-priced and seafood-focused La Cantina and the affordable, group-oriented The Village.

⊞ E10 ✉ 71 W. Monroe Street ☎ 312/332-7005
◉ Red Line: Monroe 🚌 29

LOU MITCHELL'S ($)

Longstanding Chicago diner serves fluffy omelets and homebaked pastries for which locals regularly stand in line.

⊞ E9 ✉ 565 W. Jackson Boulevard ☎ 312/939-3111
◉ Lunch only ◉ Brown, Orange Lines: Quincy 🚌 126

NINE ($$$$)

Stylish steak house serving massive steaks, as well as indulgences such as caviar and tartare.

⊞ E10 ✉ 440 W. Randolph Street ☎ 312/575-9900
◉ Closed Sun ◉ Brown Line: Washington 🚌 156

PETTERINO'S ($$$)

Supper club style restaurant that specializes in steaks and seafood. Adjacent to the Goodman Theatre this is a popular pre-curtain stop.

⊞ E9 ✉ 150 N. Dearborn Street ☎ 312/422-0150
◉ Brown, Orange Lines: Clark/Lake 🚌 156

RHAPSODY ($$$)

Adjoining Symphony Center, the elegant Rhapsody feeds music fans contemporary seafood, pastas and steaks.

⊞ F10 ✉ 65 E. Adams Street ☎ 312/786-9911
◉ No lunch Sat and Sun
◉ Brown, Orange Lines: Adams 🚌 144, 146

RUSSIAN TEA TIME ($$)

Caviar, roast pheasant, iced vodka and other Russian gastronomic specialties.

⊞ F10 ✉ 77 E. Adams Street ☎ 312/360-0000
◉ Lunch only Mon
◉ Brown, Orange Lines: Adams 🚌 1, 7, 60, 126, 151

RUTH'S CHRIS STEAKHOUSE ($$–$$$)

www.ruthschris.com
The Chicago branch of the big US steakhouse chain opened in 1992 and quickly made its mark. It serves substantial steaks, lamb, veal and

FOR VEGETARIANS

Most Chinese, Thai and Vietnamese restaurants offer meat-free versions of their staples, as do Indian eateries; Italian restaurants are another likely possibility. Even amid the chop houses and barbecued rib joints, there's usually some selection. Among the almost exclusively vegetarian restaurants try Chicago Diner (✉ 3411 N. Halsted Street ☎ 773/935-6696) and Dharma Garden Thai (✉ 3109 W. Irving Park Road ☎ 773/588-9140).

pork, all topped with sizzling butter.

⊞ E9 ✉ 431 N. Dearborn Street ☎ 312/321-2725
◉ Dinner only Sat. Closed Sun ◉ Red Line: Washington 🚌 22, 36

SEVEN ON STATE ($)

On the seventh floor of Marshall Fields, this upscale food court includes Mexican and Asian kiosks, as well as soups, salads and sandwiches.

⊞ F9 ✉ 111 N. State Street ☎ 312/781-3693 ◉ Red Line: Washington 🚌 29

SOUTH WATER KITCHEN ($$$)

Inside the Hotel Monaco, South Water Kitchen dishes up classic American fare such as macaroni and cheese and, on Friday, fried fish.

⊞ F9 ✉ 225 N. Wabash Avenue ☎ 312/236-9300
◉ Red Line: Lake; Brown, Green Orange Lines: State 🚌 29

TRATTORIA NO. 10 ($$$)

Subterranean pasta specialist near theaters draws sell-out crowds.

⊞ E9 ✉ 10 N. Dearborn Street ☎ 312/984-1718
◉ No lunch Sat; closed Sun
◉ Blue Line: Washington 🚌 29

Museum Campus

The 57-acre (23ha) lakefront Museum Campus encompasses such top cultural sights as the Adler Planetarium, Shedd Aquarium and the Field Museum with pedestrian walkways linking all three.

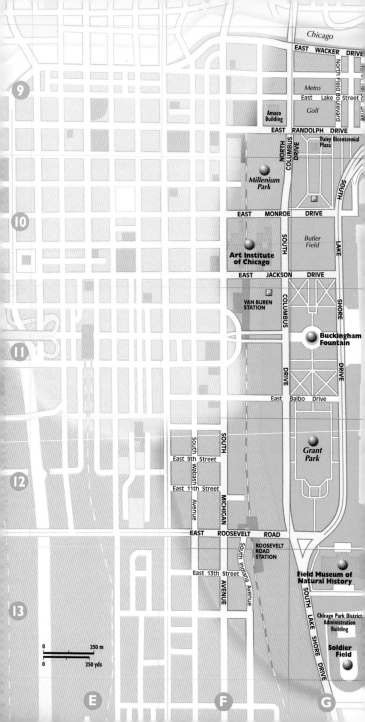

NORTH LAKE SHORE DRIVE

Monroe
Harbor

Lake

Chicago
Harbor

Michigan

John G Shedd
Aquarium

Adler Planetarium and
Astronomy Museum

P

Burnham
Park
Harbor

Northerly
Island

H   J

Adler Planetarium and Astronomy Museum

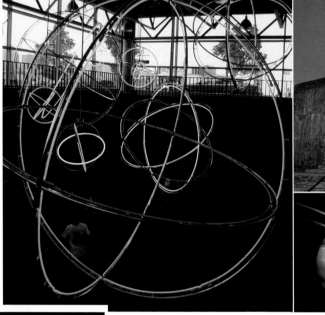

HIGHLIGHTS

- Sky Theater
- StarRider Theater
- Gateway to the Universe
- Martian rocks
- Looping 3-D film on galaxy creation

TIPS

- Expect to pay the two-show entry fee to experience the Adler in full.
- Visitors are drawn to the razzle dazzle of the StarRider Theater, but the Sky Theater's re-creation of the sky is more educational.

Projecting the night sky on an overhead dome (68ft/223m), Sky Theater has helped the Adler Planetarium and Astronomy Museum to win local hearts since it opened in 1930.

Skywatching Max Adler, a Sears Roebuck executive, realized his ambition to put the wonders of the cosmos within the reach of ordinary people when he provided the money to have the western hemisphere's first modern planetarium built in Chicago. The planetarium holds one of the world's major astronomical collections. This landmark building is a dodecahedron in rainbow granite, decorated with signs of the zodiac and topped by a lead-covered copper dome. The fascinating Sky Theater examines constellations and planets as they appear in the current night sky, projected

Clockwise from left: Detail of an exhibit; the exterior of the landmark Adler Planetarium building; details of exhibits and a relief

onto an overhead dome. The StarRider Theater uses digital technology and three-dimensional graphics to journey into space. On Friday and Saturday nights the StarRider rocks out with a musically synched computer animation show free of celestial concerns. Go on the first Friday of the month to peep through the Adler's telescopes.

Finding space Among the permanent exhibits, Universe In Your Hands documents the early earth-centered view of the universe, bolstered by a selection of medieval telescopes, and the Milky Way Galaxy offers a virtual walk through the stars. Other areas are devoted to how changing perceptions of the universe affected human culture, and the practicalities of exploring space, with items from manned exploration and samples of moon and Martian rock.

THE BASICS

www.adlerplanetarium.org

✚ H13

✉ 1300 S. Lake Shore Drive

☎ 312/322-7827

🕐 Mon–Fri 9.30–4.30, Sat–Sun 9–4.30 (1st Fri of month 9.30–10pm)

🍽 Cafeteria

Ⓞ Orange Line: Roosevelt

🚊 Roosevelt Road

🚌 146

♿ Good

💵 Expensive

Art Institute of Chicago

HIGHLIGHTS

● *Time Transfixed*, René Magritte
● *A Sunday on La Grande Jatte*, Georges Seurat
● *Paris Street; Rainy Day*, Gustave Caillebotte
● *Mother and Child*, Picasso
● *Two Sisters (on the Terrace)*, Renoir
● *American Gothic*, Grant Wood
● *Nighthawks*, Hopper

TIPS

● The institute is mobbed on weekends. If you can, visit on a weekday.
● If time-pressed, head directly for the Impressionist galleries.

Housed in a classically inspired building erected for the World's Columbian Exposition in 1893, the Art Institute has an acclaimed collection of Impressionist paintings. But its galleries showcase a lot more, from arms and armor to the original trading room of the Stock Exchange.

Masterworks Except for the celebrated *American Gothic* by Grant Wood, which is displayed amid the American collections, the pick of the paintings is the European art grouped chronologically on the ground floor. No work receives greater notice and admiration than Georges Seurat's expansive *A Sunday on La Grande Jatte*, a pointillist masterpiece. Seminal works in adjacent galleries include haystacks by

The Chicago Stock Exchange Trading Room (left); A Sunday on La Grande Jatte by Georges Seurat

Claude Monet, dancers by Edgar Degas, a self-portrait on cardboard by Vincent Van Gogh and the vibrant *Paris Street; Rainy Day* by Gustave Caillebotte. Among the many modern works are Pablo Picasso's *The Old Guitarist* and Edward Hopper's moody *Nighthawks*.

Curiosities Everything from Chinese ceramics to Guatemalan textiles has a niche on the first floor. There is a huge collection of paperweights, and there are swords, daggers and chain mail. Leave time for the stunning 1898 Trading Room of the Chicago Stock Exchange, designed by Louis Sullivan and reconstructed here. The lower level photogtraphy gallery exhibits select works from its comprehensive collection and the Thorne Miniature Rooms re-create 68 historic settings in 1-inch-to-1-foot (2.5cm-to-0.3m) scale.

THE BASICS

www.artic.edu
⊕ F10
✉ 111 S. Michigan Avenue
☎ 312/443-3600
🕐 Mon, Wed–Fri 10.30–4.30, Tue 10.30–8, Sat–Sun 10–5
🍴 Café
🚇 Brown and Orange Lines: Adams
🚌 3, 4, 60, 145, 147, 151
♿ Good
🎟 Moderate; free on Tue
❓ Free tours daily

Field Museum of Natural History

HIGHLIGHTS

- Sue
- "Traveling the Pacific"
- Dino Zone
- Gem collection
- Pawnee earth lodge
- Tibet collections
- Nature Walk

TIPS

- This vast museum requires a game plan on entry, and the menu of options often includes blockbuster touring exhibitions.
- In fair weather take a breather on the front or back steps with other picnickers.

One of the world's great natural history museums, the Field displays superb exhibits drawn from all corners of the globe. After a strenuous round of viewing, ponder the fact that only around one percent of the museum's 20 million artifacts is on display.

The building The museum was completed in 1920, its cavernous galleries providing a home for a collection originally assembled for Chicago's 1893 World's Columbian Exposition. With its porticoes, columns and beaux arts decoration, the imposing design sits rather uneasily with the needs of a modern museum, and sometimes the many rooms of exhibits from myriad eras and cultures can make for jumbled viewing. But the building's many sequestered galleries make an

Clockwise from left: Detail of a totem pole; exterior of the museum; an Albertosaurus on display; detail of ancient Egyptian art

adventure of exploring the dinosaur galleries, the taxidermy-mad Nature Walk, the life of an underground bug and corners of quirky investigation.

Great exhibits The outstanding sections include the dinosaur exhibits in which Sue, the most complete Tyrannosaurus rex ever found, takes pride of place in the entrance hall; major ancient Egyptian artifacts, spanning 5000BC to AD300, arranged in and around the dimly lighted and labyrinthine innards of a life-size, re-created tomb of a 5th-dynasty pharaoh; and "Traveling the Pacific," a powerful examination of cultural and spiritual life in Pacific cultures and the threats posed by the Western world's encroachment. Also noteworthy are the Native American displays and the gem collection, which includes pieces purchased in the 1890s from the famous Tiffany & Co jewelers.

THE BASICS

www.fieldmuseum.org

✚ G13

✉ E. Roosevelt Road at S. Lake Shore Drive

☎ 312/922-9410

🕐 Daily 9–5

🍴 Café; McDonald's

🚇 Orange Line: Roosevelt

🚋 Roosevelt Road

🚌 146

♿ Good

🎟 Moderate; free Wed

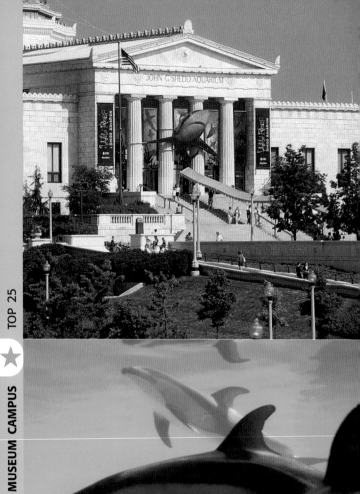

★

A Geentoo penguin (below) and a turtle (right) at the aquarium

John G. Shedd Aquarium

Chicago's "Ocean-by-the-Lake" is the world's largest indoor aquarium, enhanced by a state-of-the-art oceanarium where dolphins and whales show off typical behaviors and a Philippine reef exhibit showcasing sharks.

Aquarium A re-created Caribbean coral reef at the core of this imposing Greek-style building is home to barracuda, moray eels, nurse sharks and other creatures, who are fed several times daily by a team of microphone-equipped divers who describe the creatures, their habits and their habitat. Around the reef, denizens of the deep waters of the world occupy geographically arranged tanks. Look for the false-eye flashlight fish, born with the piscine equivalent of a flashlight.

Oceanarium Dolphins and whales are the star attractions here. Five times daily, the dolphins display natural skills such as "spy-hopping," when a dolphin raises itself onto its tail to an audience seated around a re-created chunk of Pacific Northwest coast. Winding nature trails lead to the lower-level windows that provide an underwater view of the dolphins and whales. You also see a colony of penguins, and hands-on exhibits that describe facets of sea-mammal life, such as underwater movement, respiratory system, diet, mating habits and interaction with other sea creatures. Only a 0.25-inch (0.6cm) window separates visitors from 30 sharks swimming in a massive floor-to-ceiling tank which re-creates a reef in the Philippines.

THE BASICS

www.sheddaquarium.org
✚ G12
✉ 1200 S. Lake Shore Drive
☎ 312/939-2438
🕐 Daily 9–5 (weekends until 6), Memorial Day–Labor Day 9–6
🍽 Soundings Restaurant; snacks from various stands at Bubble Net Food Court
🚇 Orange Line: Roosevelt
🚆 Roosevelt Road
🚌 146
🍽 Excellent
♿ Expensive. Aquarium free Mon and Tue Sep–end Nov; other exhibits at reduced fee

HIGHLIGHTS

- Pacific white-sided dolphins
- Beluga whales
- Sea otters
- Sea anemones
- Penguins
- Turtles
- Sharks

MUSEUM CAMPUS

TOP 25

Millennium Park

TOP 25

Jay Pritzker Pavilion *(left)* and Cloud Gate by Anish Kapoor *(below)*

MUSEUM CAMPUS   TOP 25

THE BASICS

www.millenniumpark.org
- F10
- 201 E. Randolph Drive
- 312/742-1168
- Park Grill, snack shop
- Brown, Green, Orange Lines: Randolph
- 127, 144, 146, 151
- Good
- Free

HIGHLIGHTS

- Jay Pritzker Pavilion
- *Cloud Gate*, Anish Kapoor
- The Crown Fountain
- BP Bridge
- Ice-skating rink
- Chase Promenade

This once-neglected plot (24 acres/9.7ha) of Grant Park was converted into the art-and-architecture-filled Millennium Park in 2004 to celebrate the new century, albeit four years behind schedule.

Cutting edge culture City planner Daniel Burnham put his stamp on Grant Park in the early 1900s, giving the city an apron of green at its front door. Millennium Park updates the civic respite concept with new landmarks by design-world greats including architect Frank Gehry, who brought his signature swooping-titanium style to the erection of the park's central theater, the Jay Pritzker Pavilion. Gehry also designed the winding bridge (308yd/281m) that leads park-goers lakeward. The Crown Fountain's twin glass towers (50ft/15m) project video images of a cross section of Chicagoans in portrait, while in summer children run beneath the water jets. Plazas, promenades, gardens and a restaurant with a large outdoor café in summer, provides more diversion.

The Bean Briton Anish Kapoor created the 110-ton elliptical sculpture *Cloud Gate*, known locally as "the Bean." Its highly polished surface bends and warps the surrounding skyline in reflection, a sight that commonly attracts photographers. Briefly, the city tried to block shutterbugs from capturing its image, claiming copyright infringement. Public uproar duly followed and officials relented, though the city maintains that anyone seeking to publish images of the Bean needs the permission of the artist.

More to See

BUCKINGHAM FOUNTAIN
Among the features of Grant Park is the 1926 Buckingham Fountain, notable for its computer-choreographed display of colorful lights dancing on the 1.5 million gallons (6.8 million liters) of water that are pumped daily. ⊞ G11 ✉ Grant Park

GRANT PARK
Planned by Daniel Burnham in 1909 as the centerpiece of a series of lakefront parks, Grant Park is a major festival venue that has seen everything from an infamous violence-marred 1968 anti-Vietnam War demonstration to a papal Mass in 1979. Far from being a bucolic extravaganza, Grant Park is essentially a succession of lawns crisscrossed by walkways and split in two by busy Lake Shore Drive. Bordered by the high-rises of the Loop and the expanses of Lake Michigan, Grant Park never lets you forget that you are in Chicago. Its Petrillo Music Shell provides a setting for summer concerts. ⊞ G12 ✉ Bordered by S. Michigan

Avenue, E. Randolph Drive, E. Roosevelt Road and Lake Michigan ☎ Petrillo Music Shell concert information: 312/742-4763 ◉ Visit during daylight hours only, except for special evening events ◉ Brown, Orange Lines: Randolph, Madison or Adams ▣ 3, 4, 6, 38, 60, 145, 146, 147, 151, 157

MONROE HARBOR
Some 1,000 boats moor at Monroe Harbor, just across Lake Shore Drive from Grant Park. The masts and sails provide a picturesque foreground to a lakefront stroll. ⊞ G10 ✉ Grant Park

SOLDIER FIELD
www.soldierfield.net
The original 1924 colonnaded Greek Revival stadium is home to football's Chicago Bears. A controversial 2003 addition resembling a glass-and-steel spaceship set down within the classic arcade wall updated the services of the stadium and added luxury boxes. ⊞ G13 ✉ 1410 S. Museum Drive ☎ 312/235-7000 ◉ Red Line: Roosevelt ▣ 12, 127

Skyscrapers seen above lawns crossed by walkways at Grant Park (above)

Buckingham Fountain (right)

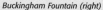

A Walk in the Park

A stroll through Chicago's front yard takes you to and past some of the city's best cultural attractions and mostly away from car traffic.

DISTANCE: Around 2 miles (3km)   **ALLOW:** 90 minutes without museum stops

START

SOLDIER FIELD (▷ 51)
🚇 Red Line: Roosevelt

1 Begin on the south end of Grant Park at Soldier Field where a classic, Greek-columned building somewhat incongruously holds a massive spaceship-shaped dish.

2 Turn north to face the back side of the Field Museum, which houses 20 million artifacts among a collection older than this 1920 building.

3 Walk north around the east side of the Field Museum. The Adler Planetarium will be lakeward to your right as is the Shedd Aquarium, the world's largest indoor such attraction.

4 Follow the Museum Campus sidewalks past the entrance of the Shedd to the promenade that skirts Monroe Harbor for a glimpse of the boats moored here each summer.

END

PARK GRILL (▷ 54)
🚇 Brown, Green, Orange Lines: Randolph

8 Stroll past the Gehry-designed stage, through the garden and catch your reflection in Anish Kapoor's mirror-like *Cloud Gate* statue. End your trip with a park-view meal at the Park Grill on the grounds.

7 Cross Monroe Drive and backtrack slightly through Grant Park to pick up the start of the Frank Gehry-designed BP Bridge, which winds its way in Millennium Park.

6 Walk north along Columbus Drive, passing the modern back side of the Art Institute of Chicago, which houses the museum's art school.

5 Continue south along Monroe Harbor, crossing Lake Shore Drive to Buckingham Fountain to see the ornate landmark with its central jet.

WALK

MUSEUM CAMPUS

52

Entertainment and Nightlife

DANCE CENTER OF COLUMBIA COLLEGE
www.dancenter.org
The 272-seat theater makes an intimate setting for productions by the Columbia dance college students; some feature internationally known artists.

➕ F13 ✉ 1306 S. Michigan Avenue ☎ 312/344-8300 🚇 Brown, Orange, Red Lines: Roosevelt 🚌 1, 3, 4

JAY PRITZKER PAVILION
www.
grantparkmusicfestival.com
Between June and August the Grant Park Music Festival holds free symphonies, jazz and pop concerts on Wednesday, Friday and Saturday

GRANT PARK'S BLUES AND JAZZ

Each June and September the Petrillo Music Shell in Grant Park (▷ 51) is the stage for blues and jazz festivals respectively, which draw top international names as well as the city's greats in both fields. The performers are greeted by tens of thousands of their admirers, who arrive with blankets and picnic supplies to enjoy the free music.

evenings. The Grant Park Orchestra and visiting guests play to 7,000 seated on the lawn and another 4,000 formally seated.

➕ G9 ✉ 205 E. Randolph Drive ☎ 312/742-7638 🚇 Brown, Green, Orange Lines: Randolph 🚌 127, 144, 146, 151

JOAN W. AND IRVING B. HARRIS THEATER FOR MUSIC AND DANCE
www.harristheaterchicago.org
The smaller of Millennium Park's entertainment venues, Harris hosts a 1,500-seat theater devoted primarily to performances of both local and visiting dance troupes.

➕ G9 ✉ 205 E. Randolph Drive ☎ 312/334-7777 🚇 Brown, Green, Orange Lines: Randolph 🚌 127, 144, 146, 151

MUSEUM CAMPUS

ENTERTAINMENT AND NIGHTLIFE

Restaurants

PRICES

Prices are approximate, based on a 3-course meal for one person.

$$$$	over $50
$$$	$31–$50
$$	$16–$30
$	up to $15

ARIA ($$$)

www.ariachicago.com
The menu at this trendy, pre-curtain spot globe-trots, offering Chicago steaks, Moroccan tagines, Asian noodle dishes and Indian naan bread.
🚇 G9 ✉ 200 N. Columbus Drive ☎ 312/444-9494
Ⓜ Brown, Green, Orange, Lines: Randolph 🚌 143, 144, 145, 146, 151

CORNER BAKERY CAFÉ ($)

Tucked just off the entry exhibit hall at the Field Museum, this cafeteria-style bakery serves pre-packaged cold and made-to-order hot sandwiches, as well as pizza slices and salads. Most dishes feature the baker's signature artisan bread.
🚇 G13 ✉ 1400 S. Lake Shore Drive ☎ 312/922-9410
Ⓜ Green, Orange, Red Lines: Roosevelt 🚌 12, 127

THE GARDEN RESTAURANT ($$)

www.artic.edu
Elegant, white-tablecloth restaurant in the heart of the Art Institute of Chicago overlooking the building's tree-filled court-yard, laying tables there in fair weather. Fancy fare includes duck confit salad and creamy risotto with mascarpone cheese.
🚇 F10 ✉ 111 S. Michigan Avenue ☎ 312/443-3600
Ⓜ Brown, Green, Orange, Lines: Adams 🚌 127, 144, 146, 151

THE PALM ($$$$)

www.thepalm.com
A gilded link in the upscale Palm steak house chain serves massive steaks and chops, catering to the who's who enshrined in caricatures on the clubby restaurant walls.
🚇 G9 ✉ 323 E. Wacker Drive ☎ 312/616-1000
Ⓜ Brown, Green, Orange Lines: Randolph 🚌 143, 144, 145, 146, 151

PARK GRILL ($$)

www.parkgrillchicago.com
Millennium Park's signature restaurant, the Park Grill overlooks the skating rink in winter and uses the outdoor pavilion for outdoor dining in summer. Lunch options focus on hamburgers, pastas and salads. Dinner features American classics like pot roast and planked salmon.
🚇 F10 ✉ 11 N. Michigan Avenue ☎ 312/521-7275
Ⓜ Brown, Green, Orange, Lines: Randolph 🚌 127, 144, 146, 151

SOUNDINGS RESTAURANT ($$)

www.sheddaquarium.org
Panoramic lake views wrap the seafood-focused sit-down restaurant at the Shedd Aquarium. Fish harvested via sustainable methods are the focus of the menu. Due to vacation crowds, only aquarium members may dine here mid-November through the New Year.
🚇 G12 ✉ 1200 S. Lake Shore Drive ☎ 312/939-2438
Ⓜ Green, Orange, Red Lines: Roosevelt 🚌 12, 127

LA STRADA RISTORANTE ($$$)

www.lastradaristorante.com
Long-standing Italian restaurant La Strada faces Millennium Park and does brisk pre-theater trade in pastas, steaks and seafood.
🚇 F10 ✉ 155 N. Michigan Avenue ☎ 312/565-2200
Ⓜ Brown, Green, Orange, Lines: Randolph 🚌 127, 144, 146

THE TASTE OF CHICAGO

Chicagoans love to eat and do so with gusto by the thousand at the Taste of Chicago festival, one of the city's most eagerly awaited events, which is held annually in Grant Park. For the 11 days before July 4 around 100 local restaurants dispense their creations at affordable prices from open-front stalls. Free musical entertainment keeps toes tapping.

Chicago's most chic shopping district, the Magnificent Mile, and priciest residential districts, including the Gold Coast, abut one another north of the Chicago River. Parks buffer the lakeshore.

Lake

Michigan

Oak Street
Beach

East Lake Shore Drive

**Hancock
Center**
East   Delaware Place
Chestnut   Street   North De
Witt Place
Lake Shore
Park
Carson   Street
Seneca
Park
AVENUE
**Museum of
Contemporary Art**

Superior   Street

North
St Clair Street
Huron   Street

CBS Studio
ONTARIO   STREET
**Weber May
Museum of Art**
useum of   STREET
ntemporary
Art
VENUE   McClurg   Court
FAIRBANKS
East   Grand

inois   Street   East   Illinois

**River-East
Museum**

COURT
North   Water   Street

Chicago   River   Drive

Outer
Harbor

Park   Drive

*Milton Lee
Olive Park*

Ohio Street
Beach

East   Ohio   Street   Park   Drive

Avenue   **Chicago
Children's
Museum**

**Chicago
Maritime
Museum**

Smith
Museum

Navy Pier

NORTH STREETER DRIVE

G   **H**   **J**

Wrigley Field exterior (below); Chicago Cubs baseball team (right)

Attending a Ball Game at Wrigley Field

The days of successive World Series wins may be a distant memory, but the baseball of the Chicago Cubs and the defiantly unmodern form of their stadium is as much a part of Chicago as the Water Tower and the El.

Landmark With its ivy-covered brick outfield wall, Wrigley Field provides the perfect setting for America's traditional pastime. Built in 1914, the stadium has steadily resisted Astroturf, and the game takes place on grass within an otherwise ordinary city neighborhood, now known as Wrigleyville. With insufficient car-parking space, most spectators have to endure densely packed El trains to reach the ballpark. General admission bleacher-seating overlooking the center field is popular at Wrigley. Dedicated Cubs fans withstand the vagaries of Chicago weather, which during the April to October season can encompass anything from snow to sunshine and 100°F (38°C) temperatures.

Tradition Nearby residents watch the game from their windows, and some convert their roof space to box-like seating and charge admission. Others rent out their driveways for parking. Above the seats is the much-loved 1937 scoreboard on which the numbers are moved not by computer chips but by human hands. The floodlights did not appear until 1988, and then only after a fierce campaign of resistance. Someone in a high place may have objected: the first night game was abandoned because of rain.

THE BASICS

⊞ Off map at D1
✉ 1060 W. Addison Street
☎ 773/404-2827
🎫 Games: Apr–early Oct
🍴 Fast-food stands; 3 restaurants
Ⓜ Red Line: Addison
🚌 22, 152
♿ Good
🎟 Tickets moderate to expensive

HIGHLIGHTS

● Outfield wall ivy
● Bleacher seats
● Glimpsing the game from the Addison El stop
● Hand-operated scoreboard
● Rooftop café overlooking Wrigleyville

NORTH SIDE

TOP 25

High Life at the Hancock

The Signature Room (left and below)

HIGHLIGHTS

- 80-mile (129km) visibility
- Views of the skyline at night
- Martini menu
- South views from the women's bathroom
- Sunset

The perfect place to toast the city skyline is from the 96th-floor cocktail lounge in one of the skyline's stars, the 1970 John Hancock Center.

The views Solid at its base and tapering as it goes skyward, the John Hancock Center, designed by the renowned firm Skidmore, Owings and Merrill and divided nearly equally between residential and commercial use, runs a paid-admission observatory on the 94th floor (www.hancock-observatory.com). But tipplers can go higher to the Signature Lounge on the 96th floor, reached via a separate elevator with no admission charge. On a clear day visitors can see 80 miles (129km) and four surrounding states from the perch over Oak Street Beach. With unreserved seating, patrons have to dash for the best windowside seats when they become available, though all the tables have good sightlines. Sunsets draw a crowd, but it's really after sundown when the lights come up in spires all around you that the lounge is at its most romantic.

The libations Patrons of the Signature Lounge pay for the view with high-price drinks—the Michigan Avenue Martini runs $11, wines go for $11 to $14 per glass. Sandwiches and appetizers such as shrimp cocktail and cheese plates ($10 to $12) aim to keep you seated for round two or more. For a full meal, stop one floor down where the Signature Room at the 95th provides similar views.

The Roy Boyd Gallery (below); exterior of Carl Hammer Gallery (right)

Gallery Hopping in River North

Dozens of art dealers occupy the former warehouses in River North's most handsome district for one-stop art shopping. Tours of galleries happen on Saturday.

From industry to art Chicago's gallery district claims roughly 70 art sellers in the heart of River North bounded by Chicago Avenue on the north, the Chicago River on the south, La Salle to the east and Orleans to the west. The area boomed with industry beginning in the 1890s when railroad tracks lined the north bank of the Chicago River, earning it the nickname "Smokey Hollow." River North slid slowly into decay as factories gradually closed in the 1950s and '60s. In the 1970s, attracted by low rents and large spaces, artists began to move in. Later, galleries followed, cementing the art scene in the district of redbrick warehouse buildings. Chain restaurants and residential condos have more recently driven up rents in the area, but the galleries clustered on Huron and Superior streets in particular have managed to survive the real-estate rush.

Art scene The most established artists showing in Chicago exhibit here alongside national and international names. Maya Polsky Gallery shows works by the late Ed Paschke, Roy Boyd Gallery exhibits the abstract oils of Dan Devening and Carl Hammer Gallery displays Mr. Imagination, whose medium is bottle caps. All are open to the public but to visit with a guide, show up at Starbuck's at 750 N. Franklin Street at 11am any Saturday where the free tours kick off.

THE BASICS

🔲 D7

✉ Between the Chicago River and Chicago Avenue, La Salle and Orleans streets

🕐 Gallery hours vary; most open Tue–Sat 10–6

🍴 Restaurants, cafés and coffee shops nearby

Ⓑ Brown Line: Chicago

🚌 66

♿ Good

🎟 Free

HIGHLIGHTS

● Roy Boyd Gallery
● Carl Hammer Gallery
● Robert Henry James
Fine Art
● Byron Roche Gallery
● Zolla/Lieberman Gallery
● Maya Polsky Gallery

NORTH SIDE ★ **TOP 25**

61

Lincoln Park Zoo

HIGHLIGHTS

- Regenstein African Journey
- Regenstein Center for African Apes
- Kovler Sea Lion Pool
- Swimming polar bears
- Endangered Species Carousel
- Farm-in-the-Zoo

TIPS

- For one of the more entertaining events at the zoo, plan to arrive at the sea lion pool for the 2pm feeding.

Free to the public and a city block from a popular residential district, the zoo is a local favorite showcasing wild animals as well as a dairy farm, itself an endangered species in the Midwest.

Small beginnings Created out of sand dunes, swamp and the former city cemetery, Lincoln Park was established by the 1870s after its zoo had been started with the gift of two swans from New York's Central Park. Evolving over several years through the contributions of various designers, it is the oldest and most visited park in the country.

Wild kingdom The zoo, a block east of a smart residential district, is very much a part of city life where passersby can drop in on the lion pride or the swimming polar bears. Early-20th-century brick

Clockwise from left: A polar bear cooling off; the chimpanzee enclosure; giraffe; observing the seals; a tiger and a gorilla

buildings house the big cats, small mammals and some monkeys, but a spate of new building has brought more immersive exhibits to the zoo. The Regenstein African Journey creates an atmospheric passage through habitats for pygmy hippos, deer-like klipspringers, wild dogs, towering giraffes and even cockroaches. The new Regenstein Center for African Apes lets the light shine into vine-covered and bamboo-planted indoor living areas, supplemented by outdoor grounds. The Children's Zoo combines play in a climbing area and education with interactive exhibits.

Down on the farm Farm-in-the-Zoo's white-trimmed red barn is one of Chicago's more unusual buildings. The farmyard attempts to teach kids where food comes from with daily presentations on milking, butter-churning and egg hatching.

THE BASICS

www.lpzoo.com
✚ E2
✉ 2001 N. Clark Street
☎ 312/742-2000
🕐 Daily 9–6
Ⓑ Brown Line: Fullerton
🚌 151, 156
♿ Good
🆓 Free

Navy Pier

HIGHLIGHTS

- Ferris wheel
- Chicago Children's Museum
- Chicago Shakespeare Theater
- Boat rides
- Stained-glass window exhibit
- Views of city from the end of the pier

TIPS

- The little-known beer garden at the end of the pier serves draft beer, snacks and a lineup of local bands in summer with great skyline views.

Few visitor attractions anywhere in the world have a collection of stained-glass windows vying for attention with a 15-story Ferris wheel, but at Navy Pier they do just that, part of an expanding venue that mixes culture, cuisine, entertainment and retail.

History and cruises Opened in 1916, Navy Pier was part of architect Daniel Burnham's vision for a new Chicago and was intended to combine shipping with dining and entertainment. The former steadily disappeared and the pier declined until a 1990s makeover saw it reemerge as a stylish family-aimed entertainment venue in the heart of the city. The pier has encouraged a revival of water activity with a plethora of pleasure cruises departing from its edge along Dock Street.

Clockwise from left: Walking along Navy Pier; looking toward Navy Pier with its Ferris wheel; Smith Museum of Stained Glass on Navy Pier; fountain outside the Children's Museum

Entertainment For thrills and spills, try Time Escape, a 3-D ride catapulting you from the present back to the Lake Michigan of 85 million BC and forward to Chicago in the 24th century. The daring can ride the Wave Swinger's motorized swings spinning 14ft (4m) off the floor, while the placid can enjoy the miniature golf course.

Culture For intellectual balance get tickets to the acclaimed Chicago Shakespeare Theater, modeled on the venues of the Bard's own day with seating surrounding the stage on three levels. Exactly 150 stained-glass windows line the pier hallways, comprising the Smith Museum of Stained Glass Windows with superior selections by Louis Comfort Tiffany as well as Prairie School-era works. The Chicago Children's Museum educates as it entertains (▷ 69).

THE BASICS

www.navypier.com
🚇 H8
✉ 600 E. Grand Avenue
☎ 312/595-7437
🕐 Summer: Fri–Sat 10am–midnight, Sun–Thu 10–10; shorter hours in winter
🍴 Various restaurants and cafés
Ⓡ Red Line: Grand
🚌 29, 56, 65, 66
♿ Good
🆓 Free; fee for individual attractions

North Avenue Beach

Outdoor activities at North Avenue Beach

THE BASICS

www.
chicagoparkdistrict.com

✚ F4

✉ 1603 N. Lake Shore Drive

☎ 312/742-7529

🚇 Red Line: Clark Street

🚌 72

♿ Fair

✋ Free

HIGHLIGHTS

● Beach volleyball
● Chess Pavilion
● Ocean-liner bathhouse
● Upper-deck Castaways Bar & Grill
● Seasonal outdoor gym
● Swimming

Daily in summer, and especially on weekends and holidays, Chicagoans storm this beach, one of the liveliest and best equipped of the city's 33 strands on the 31-mile (50km) Lake Michigan shore.

Games for all For a look at Chicagoans of every stripe and how they relax, head to North Avenue Beach, a community playground for families, young singles, exercise fanatics and sybarites. The park is known as a volleyballer's delight, lined with net uprights (players provide the nets and balls) used by teams as well as casual pick-up players. A temporary stadium showcases professional players when they come to town in July. Brainy sorts head to the Chess Pavilion on the concrete biking and walking path south of the beach. Each summer a seasonal outdoor gym provides weights and exercise equipment for the body proud. While you can watch Chicago's annual August Air and Water Show from a number of beaches up and down the shore, the main action takes place at North Avenue, drawing the lion's share of the million people a day who view the boat and airplane displays.

Bathhouse The ocean-liner-looking building beached on the shore replaced the original landmark Depression-era bathhouse of the same design. The 2000 version has showers, restrooms and concession stands as well as beach chair, bike and volleyball equipment rentals. Singles go to Castaways Bar & Grill for margaritas and beer, though it serves salads and sandwiches.

Detail of the exterior (below); outside the theater (center and right)

Second City

From the stage at Second City, Chicago performers, including some very famous cast members, popularized a form of improvised comedy now seen on television and in cities around the world.

Their laurels Chicago's signature brand of bold, broad and quick wit was nurtured and became popular at Second City. Since 1959 the Old Town comedy theater has been training actors such as original *Saturday Night Live* cast members John Belushi, Bill Murray and Gilda Radner. Other alumni who have passed through the theater and on to lucrative film gigs include Dan Ackroyd, Mike Myers of *Austin Powers* fame and *Ghostbusters* director Harold Ramis. Shows bear names like "Iraqtile Dysfunction" and "Truth, Justice, or the American Way," riffing on current events, pop culture and the American political scene.

Improv comedy Improvisational comedy uses no script, relying instead on the actors to supply the dialog and the direction. They call for audience suggestions and incorporate those into the action in a form known as "spot improv," popular at Second City. Theater historians trace improv back to early Europe's Commedia del'Arte in which theater troupes traveled from town to town performing in public squares and improvising the script based on a theme. With thought to making theater more generally accessible, a group of actors founded The Compass in 1950s' Chicago, which later became Second City and went on to influence performers worldwide.

THE BASICS

www.secondcity.com

⊞ E4

✉ 161 N. Wells Street

☎ 312/337-3992

🕐 Tue–Thu 8, Fri–Sat 8 and 11, Sun 7

🚇 Red Line: Clark Street

🚌 72, 156

♿ Fair

💰 Moderate

HIGHLIGHTS

● Improv shows
● Cabaret seating
● Two stages
● Central Old Town location near restaurants and bars

Shopping the Magnificent Mile

Shoppers orienting themselves and walking (left and right); Tiffany's (middle)

THE BASICS

www.
themagnificentmile.com

✚ F8

✉ Michigan Avenue north of the Chicago River to its terminus at Oak Street

☎ 312/642-3570

Ⓡ Red Line: Chicago, Grand

🚌 143, 144, 145, 146, 151

♿ Good

HIGHLIGHTS

● Water Tower and Pumping Station
● Bloomingdale's
● Nordstrom
● Saks Fifth Avenue
● Crate & Barrel
● Ralph Lauren

From the Chicago River to Oak Street Beach, that portion of Michigan Avenue known as Chicago's Magnificent Mile lines up designer boutiques and major department stores in one bustling stretch.

Shop till you drop Some 460 stores pack the mile, selling something for everyone from designer goods by Salvatore Ferragamo, precious jewelry at Cartier and the tailored suits of Brooks Brothers to off-price fashions from T. J. Maxx and Swedish retailer H&M. Between high and low ends are the major American department stores, including Nordstrom, known for its quality clothes and deep shoe selection; Neiman Marcus, famed for its exclusive clientele and designer racks; and Bloomingdale's with trendy looks for each family member. Vertical malls such as 900 North Michigan, which houses Bloomingdale's and Water Tower Place, home to the former Marshal Fields, now Macy's, house specialty shops such as cook's favorite Williams-Sonoma in the former and funky accessorist Chiasso at the latter.

Culture breaks Architectural icons line the street, making this a good walk even for the shop shy. The Wrigley Building and the Chicago Tribune Building face off against one another on the south end of the street. Farther north, the historic Water Tower and Pumping Station, two of the few to survive the Great Fire of 1871, symbolize the rebirth of the city on the prosperous thoroughfare. A block from Michigan Avenue, the Museum of Contemporary Art shows cutting-edge work.

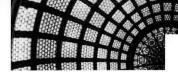

More to See

BOY'S TOWN

www.northalsted.com

The pocket of Lakeview around North Halsted Street from Belmont north to Addison is the locus of the gay community in Chicago, with a lively collection of bars, shops and restaurants.
➕ Off map at C1 ✉ Halsted Street from Belmont north to Addison 🚇 Red Line: Belmont Addison; Brown Line: Belmont 🚌 8, 77 ♿ Good

CHICAGO CHILDREN'S MUSEUM

www.childrensmuseum.org

Three floors of scores of lively and entertaining things to do for those aged under 12. These include workshop areas such as the Inventing Lab, where children can assemble flying machines, and Artabounds where they can create their own murals and sculptures. Programs change daily.
➕ H8 ✉ Navy Pier, 700 E. Grand Avenue ☎ 312/527-1000 🕐 Sun–Wed, Fri 10–5, Thu, Sat 10–4, 5–8 🚇 Red Line: Grand 🚌 29, 56, 65, 66 ♿ Good ✋ Moderate; free Thu 5–8

CHICAGO HISTORICAL SOCIETY

www.chicagohs.org

In a Georgian-style brick building constructed in 1932, with a modern, glass-walled extension, every major facet in Chicago's rise from swampland to metropolis is discussed and illustrated in chronologically arranged galleries. Alongside temporary shows, the American Wing houses exhibitions that explore US history via informative texts and excellent period items.
➕ E4–E5 ✉ 1601 N. Clark Street ☎ 312/642-4600 🕐 Mon–Sat 9.30–4.30 🚇 Brown Line: Sedgwick 🚌 11, 22, 36, 72, 151, 156 ♿ Good ✋ Inexpensive; free Mon

FOURTH PRESBYTERIAN CHURCH (1914)

www.fourthchurch.org

This Gothic Revival church serves a congregation of Chicago's moneyed élite. Occasional but enjoyable lunchtime concerts pack the pews.
➕ F7 ✉ 126 E. Chestnut Street ☎ 312/787-4570 🚇 Red Line: Chicago 🚌 145, 146, 147, 151 ♿ Good

Chicago Children's Museum (above)

Rail tickets displayed at Chicago Historical Society (right)

THE GOLD COAST

In the late 19th century, Chicago businessman Potter Palmer astonished his peers by erecting a mansion home on undeveloped land well north of the Loop close to Lake Michigan. As others followed, the area became known as the Gold Coast, its streets lined by the elegant homes of the well-to-do.
✚ F5

GRACELAND CEMETERY

www.gracelandcemetery.org
Graceland is Chicago's most prestigious cemetery. Alongside great Chicagoans are a host of others, famous and infamous. City architect Louis Sullivan has left a mark with his ornate 1890 tomb for the steel magnate Henry Getty and his family. Sullivan is here, as are other Chicago architects Daniel Burnham, John Root and modernist Ludwig Mies van der Rohe. The free map from the office is essential.
✚ Off map at D1 ✉ 4001 N. Clark Street
☎ 312/525-1105 ⏰ Office: Mon–Sat 8.30–4.30. Gates: 8–6.30 🚇 Brown Line: Irving Park. Red Line: Sheridan 🚌 80
♿ Good 🖐 Free

HISTORIC WATER TOWER (1869)

This pseudo-Gothic confection in yellow limestone, by William Boyington, is a city landmark.
✚ F7 ✉ 806 N. Michigan Avenue
☎ First-floor photography gallery: 312/742-0808 ⏰ Mon–Sat 10–6.30, Sun 10–5
🚇 Red Line: Chicago 🚌 11, 66, 145, 146, 147, 151 ♿ Few 🖐 Free

HOLY NAME CATHEDRAL (1878)

www.holynamecathedral.com
This is the atmospheric seat of the Catholic Archdiocese of Chicago. Bullets from the 1926 gangland murder of mobster "Hymie" Weiss chipped the building's cornerstone.
✚ F7 ✉ 735 N. State Street ☎ 312/787-8040 🚇 Red Line: Chicago 🚌 29, 36
♿ Good

INTERNATIONAL MUSEUM OF SURGICAL SCIENCES

www.imss.org
The museum's several floors, as well

The Hall of Mortals at the International Museum of Surgical Sciences (above)

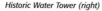

Historic Water Tower (right)

as innovative temporary shows, cover health and medicine-related subjects. Among the oldest exhibits are drilled skulls from Peruvian temples, and surgeon's tools found in excavations at the Roman town of Pompeii. Many rooms are packed with displays of fearsome needles, hooks and other sharp metallic things.

✚ F5 ✉ 1524 N. Lake Shore Drive ☎ 312/642-6502 ⏰ Tue–Sat 10–4 (also May–Sep Sun 10–4) 🚇 Brown Line: Sedgwick 🚌 151 ♿ Good 💵 Moderate ❓ Guided tour Sat 2pm

LINCOLN PARK CONSERVATORY

The Conservatory (1891) encompasses four separate greenhouses. Invitingly warm on cool and breezy Chicago days, the greenhouses provide balmy temperatures for dazzling tropical and subtropical blooms and seasonal displays.

✚ E2 ✉ 2391 N. Stockton Drive ☎ Conservatory: 312/742-7736 ⏰ Daily 9–5 ♿ Good 🚇 Red Line: Armitage 🚌 76, 77, 145, 146, 147, 151, 156 💵 Free

MUSEUM OF CONTEMPORARY ART

www.mcachicago.org

Highlights from the permanent collection include the works of the Chicago-based Ed Paschke, and Richard Long's *Chicago Mud Circle* (1996), created directly on a gallery wall. The lower levels house temporary exhibitions and provide access to the Sculpture Garden.

✚ F7 ✉ 220 E. Chicago Avenue ☎ 312/280-2660 ⏰ Tue 10–8, Wed–Sun 10–5 🍴 Café 🚇 Red Line: Chicago 🚌 157 ♿ Good 💵 Moderate; free on Tue 5–8

OAK STREET BEACH

The closeness of the exclusive Gold Coast neighborhood helps make Oak Street Beach the gathering place for some of Chicago's richest and best-toned bodies.

✚ F6 ✉ Access from junction of N. Michigan Avenue and E. Lake Shore Drive 🚌 145, 146, 147, 151

Bust of the conductor Sir Georg Solti outside the Conservatory in Lincoln Park

OLD TOWN

www.oldtownchicago.org

Gentrified in the 1960s and '70s by artists, Old Town combines restaurant-lined commercial throughways and intimate leafy residential streets. The annual June art fair is a big draw.

➕ D5 ✉ Streets fan out from intersection of North Avenue and Wells Street 🚇 Brown Line: Sedgwick 🚌 11, 72, 156

THE PEGGY NOTEBAERT NATURE MUSEUM

www.naturemuseum.org

Lively exhibits explore the natural history of the Midwest, including a greenhouse holding Butterfly Haven, and the inside story on the insect population of every household.

➕ E2 ✉ On banks of North Pond in Lincoln Park ☎ 773/755-5100 🕐 Mon–Fri 9–4.30, Sat–Sun 10–5 🚇 Brown and Red Lines: Fullerton 🚌 22, 36, 72, 156 ♿ Good 🖐 Inexpensive; free Thu

THE TRIBUNE TOWER

In the 1920s, the *Chicago Tribune* staged a competition for the design of its new premises. The resulting neo-Gothic building is best admired from the exterior, inlaid with 120 stones from sites around the world including Greece's Parthenon and India's Taj Mahal. You can watch WGN, the *Tribune*-owned radio station, through the studio window.

➕ F8 ✉ 435 N. Michigan Avenue ☎ 312/222-3994 🚇 Red Line: Grand 🚌 3, 11, 29, 65, 147, 151, 157 ♿ Good

THE WRIGLEY BUILDING

The Wrigley Building was partly modeled on the Giralda Tower in Seville, Spain, although the ornamental features echo the French Renaissance. The North and South buildings stand behind a continuous facade linked by an arcaded walkway at street level and by two enclosed aerial walkways. The ornate glazed terra-cotta facade has retained its original gleam; most effective when illuminated at night.

➕ F8 ✉ 400 N. Michigan Avenue ☎ 312/923-8080 🕐 Business hours 🚇 Red Line: Grand 🚌 3, 11, 29, 65, 147, 151, 157 ♿ Good 🖐 Free

The Wrigley Building (above)

The ornate entrance to the Tribune Tower (right)

One Magnificent Walk

Take in several architectural icons as well as the glitziest shopping in a mile-long walk up Michigan Avenue from the Chicago River.

DISTANCE: 1 mile (1.6 km) **ALLOW:** 2–3 hours

START

MICHIGAN AVENUE BRIDGE
🚇 Red Line: Grand 🚌 3, 11, 29, 65, 147, 151, 157

END

JOHN HANCOCK CENTER (▷ 60)
🚇 Red Line: Chicago 🚌 145, 146, 147, 151

1 Leave the Loop by walking north across the Chicago River on Michigan Avenue Bridge, which in 1920 facilitated the rise of the so-called Magnificent Mile.

8 Finish the walk at the John Hancock Center (1970), whose 94th-floor observatory affords stunning views across Chicago.

2 Two of the first structures erected after the bridge was built were the Wrigley Building (1921–24), to the left, and the Tribune Tower (1925), to the right.

7 A short distance west, on Chestnut Street, there is more Gothic exuberance at the Quigley Seminary (1920s). Return to and cross Michigan Avenue to Water Tower Place, a glitzy, high-profile shopping mall.

3 Farther north, opulent shops and hotels line Michigan Avenue. One of the liveliest stores is Nike Town between Erie and Huron streets.

6 The water tower survived a fire and now holds a photographic gallery. A block north, on the junction with Chestnut Street, is the imposing Gothic form of the Fourth Presbyterian Church, used for lunchtime recitals.

4 Cross to the west side of Michigan Avenue for a bag of cheese popcorn from Garrett Popcorn, at 670 N.Michigan Avenue.

5 Continue to the junction with Chicago Avenue and stop at the Historic Water Tower.

NORTH SIDE

WALK

Shopping

AFTER-WORDS

New titles on most subjects, but leaning toward less-than-mainstream fiction, politics and history; plus lots of used books.
🕀 E8 ✉ 23 E. Illinois Street ☎ 312/464-1110 🚇 Red Line: Grand 🚌 22, 29, 36

BANANA REPUBLIC

www.bananarepublic.com
Popular local branch of the supplier of quality casualwear.
🕀 F8 ✉ 744 N. Michigan Avenue ☎ 312/642-0020 🚇 Red Line: Chicago 🚌 145, 146, 147, 151

BARNEYS NEW YORK

www.barneys.com
Branch of a Manhattan store noted for chic women's clothing and its fine menswear.
🕀 F6 ✉ 25 E. Oak Street ☎ 312/587-1700 🚇 Red Line: Chicago 🚌 145, 146, 147, 151

BROOKS BROTHERS

www.brooksbrothers.com
Well-made menswear, in conservative styles, plus some equally straightforward clothing for women.
🕀 F8 ✉ 713 N. Michigan Avenue ☎ 312/915-0060 🚇 Red Line: Chicago 🚌 145, 146, 147, 151

CHICAGO PLACE

www.chicago-place.com
A seven-floor branch of Saks Fifth Avenue department store is an anchor tenant among the classy retailers in this towering construction. There's a food hall on the top floor.

🕀 F8 ✉ 700 N. Michigan Avenue ☎ 312/266-7710 🚇 Red Line: Chicago 🚌 145, 146, 147, 151

THE DAISY SHOP

www.daisyshop.com
Gloves, handkerchiefs and jewelry feature among the used designer accessories; shelves of flowing chiffon dresses.
🕀 F6 ✉ 67 E. Oak Street ☎ 312/943-8880 🚇 Red Line: Chicago 🚌 145, 146, 147, 151

J. CREW

www.jcrew.com
Classic modern clothes, shoes and accessories for young men and women at work and play.
🕀 F7 ✉ 900 N. Michigan Avenue ☎ 312/751-2739 🚇 Red Line: Chicago 🚌 145, 146, 147, 151

NATIONAL CHAINS

The Diversey branch of Barnes & Noble (✉ 659 W. Diversey Parkway ☎ 773/871-9004 🚇 Brown line: Diversey 🚌 22, 36, 76) is a superstore, with shelf after shelf of general titles, newspapers and magazines, in an atmosphere conducive to browsing. Borders Books & Music (✉ 830 N. Michigan Avenue ☎ 312/573-0564 🚇 Red line: Chicago 🚌 145, 146, 147, 151) has a comparably huge selection. Both have cafés.

LORD & TAYLOR

www.lordandtaylor.com
Lovely, classic clothes, shoes and accessories for men and women.
🕀 F7 ✉ Water Tower Place, 835 N. Michigan Avenue ☎ 312/787-7400 🚇 Red Line: Chicago 🚌 145, 146, 147, 151

NAVY PIER

www.navypier.com
Some 60 shops are gathered in this complex of restaurants and entertainment. If you want souvenirs as gifts, this is a good place.
🕀 H8 ✉ 700 E. Grand Avenue ☎ 312/595-7437 🚇 Red Line: Grand 🚌 29, 56, 65, 66

NEIMAN-MARCUS

www.neimanmarcus.com
Exclusive, elegant clothing is the forte of this store which also sells beauty products and fancy food stuffs. Just looking is good fun.
🕀 F8 ✉ 737 N. Michigan Avenue ☎ 312/642-5900 🚇 Red Line: Chicago 🚌 145, 146, 147, 151

900 NORTH MICHIGAN

www.shop900.com
This gleaming marble high-rise consumes a city block. Restaurants, cinemas and stores are grouped around a six-floor atrium; a branch of Bloomingdale's is an anchor. There are also smaller, exclusive stores.
🕀 F7 ✉ 900 N. Michigan

Avenue 312/915-3916
Red Line: Chicago
145, 146, 147, 151

P.O.S.H.
www.poshchicago.com
The expression "port out/starboard home" used by aristocrats seeking the shady side of the ship journeying between Britain and India lends its name to this antiques shop specializing in vintage tabletop items from the early 19th century.
F8 613 N. State Street
312/280-1602 Red Line: Grand
22, 65

PRADA
www.prada.com
Three levels of clothing and accessories.
F6 30 E. Oak Street
312/951-1113 Red Line: Chicago 145, 146, 147, 151

RAND MCNALLY MAP STORE
www.randmcnally.com
Atlases, maps and guidebooks.
F7 444 N. Michigan Avenue 312/321-1751
Red Line: Grand 3, 11, 145, 146, 147, 151

R. H. LOVE GALLERIES
www.rhgalleries.com
For decades Chicago's leading purveyor of fine American paintings and prints; even if the purchase of an original is beyond your means, admire the displays and

frequent exhibitions.
F7 2nd floor, 645 N. Michigan Avenue
800/437-7568 Red Line: Grand 3, 11, 125, 145, 146, 147, 151

SHOPS AT THE MART
www.merchandisemart.com
Most of the vast Merchandise Mart is closed to the public, except for the first two floors, which woo shoppers with clothing stores, gift shops and food court.
E9 350 N. Wells Street
Brown, Purple Lines: Merchandise Mart 37

SUGAR MAGNOLIA
www.sugarmagnolia.com
Cheerful shop for women's casual clothing with a bohemian bent.
F6 34 E. Oak Street
312/944-0885 Red Line: Chicago 22, 143, 145, 146, 151

MAGNIFICENT MILE

No Chicago shopper could be unaware that most top-class stores are gathered along the section of Michigan Avenue known as the Magnificent Mile. Many stores appeared here following the 1920s opening of the river bridge linking Michigan Avenue to the Loop, but the "Magnificent Mile" concept was a 1940s idea that eventually mutated into today's rows of marble-clad towers, mostly built during the 1970s and 1980s.

ULTIMO
www.ultimo.com
Chic boutique with a well-edited designer selection dresses the city's fashionistas.
F6 114 E. Oak Street
312/787-11713 Red Line: Chicago 145, 146, 147, 151

WATER TOWER PLACE
www.shopwatertower.com
Packing these seven floors are clothing stores for men, women and children that span Abercrombie & Fitch, North Beach Leather, Baby Gap and Victoria's Secret. There are also jewelers, art galleries, home-furnishing emporiums, cinemas and restaurants, and specialty retailers such as Accent Chicago and the Water Tower Clock Shop.
F7 835 N. Michigan Avenue 312/440-3165
Red Line: Chicago 145, 146, 147, 151

WESTFIELD NORTH BRIDGE
www.westfield.com/northbridge
Another Magnificent Mile mall, this one includes branches of AIX Armani, Body Shop and Spa Nordstrom, and several children's stores.
F7 520 N. Michigan Avenue 312/327-3200
Red Line: Chicago 145, 146, 147, 15

Entertainment and Nightlife

ANDY'S JAZZ CLUB

www.jazzclub.com
Popular and unpretentious jazz venue that earns its keep by staging commendable sets on weekday lunchtimes, as well as early and mid-evening shows.

F8 ⊠ 11 E. Hubbard Street ☎ 312/642-6805 Red Line: Grand 29, 36

BILLY GOAT TAVERN

www.billygoattavern.com
This below-street-level, unpretentious watering hole is a favorite among local journalists.

F8 ⊠ 430 N. Michigan Avenue ☎ 312/222-1525 Red Line: Grand 145, 146, 147, 151

BLUE CHICAGO

www.bluechicago.com
Comfortable, homey blues club, showcasing home-grown musical talent.

E7 ⊠ 736 N. Clark Street ☎ 312/642-6261 Red Line: Chicago 22, 36

CHICAGO SHAKESPEARE THEATER

www.chicagoshakes.com
A 500-seat auditorium raised at a cost of $24 million makes a splendid setting for the works of the Bard. Abridged "Short Shakespeare" and family musicals fill the stage in summer.

H8 ⊠ 600 E. Grand Avenue ☎ 312/596-5600 Red Line: Grand 29, 56, 65, 66

EXCALIBUR

www.excaliburchicago.com
This complex of billiards, pinball, video games, discos and a restaurant is incongruously set in a 19th-century pseudo-Gothic castle, a sturdy granite structure built in the 1890s for the Chicago Historical Society. A favorite with twenty-somethings.

E8 ⊠ 632 N. Dearborn Street ☎ 312/266-1944 Red Line: Grand 22

HOUSE OF BLUES

www.hob.com
Blues and rock from around the city, the country and the world every night. The smaller Back Porch stage has blues nightly and is open at lunch for more of the same. A gospel choir stars at Sunday brunch.

E9 ⊠ 329 N. Dearborn Street ☎ 312/923-2000 Red Line: Grand 22, 36, 62

NIGHTCLUB NEWS

The most general source is the Friday edition of the *Chicago Tribune* and its Metromix website (www.metromix.com). Inside info on the latest clubs, as well as the nightlife scene in general, can be found in the pages of the weekly *Chicago Reader* and *New City*, both free of charge, and on their websites. The weekly magazine *Time Out Chicago* is sold on local newsstands.

JAZZ SHOWCASE

www.jazzshowcase.com
Photos of jazz legends decorate this historic joint, and big names in contemporary jazz play here. Bring the kids to the Sunday matinee performances.

E8 ⊠ 59 W. Grand Avenue ☎ 312/670-2473 Red Line: Grand 22, 65

JOE'S BE-BOP CAFÉ

www.joesbebop.com
Listen to be-bop and other jazz while tucking into jambalaya, barbecued ribs and other cajun dishes. Popular among music fans and tourists alike.

H8–J8 ⊠ Navy Pier, 700 E. Grand Avenue ☎ 312/595-5299 Red Line: Grand 29, 55, 65, 66

KAZ BAR

www.kazbarchicago.com
Attempts to re-create Morocco in Chicago are rare and this gloriously kitsch rendition of the Kasbah is worth a look. If the plush sofas fail to appeal, sip your cocktail inside a tent.

E9 ⊠ House of Blues Hotel, 333 N. Dearborn Street ☎ 312/245-0333 Red Line: Grand 22, 36, 62

LOOKINGGLASS THEATER

www.lookingglasstheater.com
Housed in the Water Tower Pumping Station, the Lookingglass troupe is lauded for its experimental staging and frequent

use of circus arts.
🔁 F7 ✉ 821 N. Michigan Avenue ☎ 312/337-0665 🚇 Red Line: Chicago 🚌 66, 143, 144, 145, 146, 151

PARK WEST

www.parkwestchicago.com
Intimate size and strong acoustics make this the ideal place for non-ear-splitting music, be it folk, jazz, rock or something else from the eclectic itinerary.
🔁 D3 ✉ 322 W. Armitage Avenue ☎ 773/929-5959 🚇 Brown or Red Lines: Armitage 🚌 23, 72

LE PASSAGE

The well-heeled toddle down a cobblestone alley to reach the subterranean Le Passage, a swank drinking and dancing nightspot with a celebrity following.
🔁 F7 ✉ 537 N. Rush Street ☎ 312/255-0022 🚇 Red Line: Chicago 🚌 22, 66

SECOND CITY

www.secondcity.com
Biting satire and inspired improvisation have long been the stock-in-trade here, and they have been so successful that a second Second City theater now offers a different show simultaneously.
▷ 67.
🔁 E5 ✉ 1616 N. Wells Street ☎ 773/337-3992 🚇 Brown Line: Sedgwick 🚌 11, 156

SPY BAR

www.spybarchicago.com
Patrons dress in swanky club gear to edge past the bouncers, then sip Martinis before grooving to house music—the Spy Bar specialty. Sink into a velvet couch when you need a breather. Entrance through alleyway.
🔁 E7 ✉ 646 N. Franklin Street ☎ 312/587-8779 🚇 Brown Line: Chicago 🚌 37

STEPPENWOLF THEATER

www.steppenwolf.org
Home of the enormously successful and influential Steppenwolf repertory company, founded in 1976, and still a premier venue for the best of Off-Loop theater. The theater has a 900-seat main hall and a smaller space for experimental drama. High-profile members include movie star John Malkovich.
🔁 C4 ✉ 1650 N. Halsted Street ☎ 312/335-3830 🚇 Red Line: North/Clybourn 🚌 8, 72

STONE LOTUS

www.stonelotuslounge.com
High fashion River North club specializing in bottle

service that comes with food planned to match the booze. Expect celebrities, models and expensive tabs.
🔁 D7 ✉ 873 N. Orleans Street ☎ 312/440-9680 🚇 Brown Line: Chicago 🚌 66

SYN

www.synchicago.com
Futuristic/minimalist decor with a hint of decadence sets the tone for one of the city's newest and most upscale nightspots; the first choice for champagne-sipping clubbers.
🔁 F7 ✉ 1009 N. Rush Street ☎ 312/664-1001 🚇 Red Line: Chicago 🚌 36

10 PIN BOWLING LOUNGE

www.10pinchicago.com
The stodgy sport of bowling gets glammed up at this 24-lane venue, with video art on the walls and martinis on the menu.
🔁 E9 ✉ 330 N. State Street ☎ 312/644-0300 🚇 Red Line: Grand 🚌 22, 29

ZANIES

www.zanies.com
Small, enjoyable comedy club, featuring rising local stars as well as better-known names.
🔁 E5 ✉ 1548 N. Wells Street ☎ 312/337-4027 🚇 Brown Line: Sedgwick 🚌 11, 156

Restaurants

PRICES

Prices are approximate, based on a 3-course meal for one person.

$$$$	over $50
$$$	$31–$50
$$	$16–$30
$	up to $15

ADOBO GRILL ($$)

www.adobogrill.com
Authentic Mexican dishes in a convivial atmosphere just below Second City. Don't miss the guacamole, prepared tableside. Connoisseurs choose from more than 100 tequilas on offer.

➕ E5 ✉ 1610 N. Wells Street ☎ 312/266-7999 Ⓜ Red Line: Clark/Division 🚌 72, 156

ALINEA ($$$$)

www.alinea-restaurant.com
Chef Grant Achatz practices a form of alchemical cooking at Alinea that incorporates science in deconstructing dishes presented on custom serving pieces such as spindles or aromatic pillows. For bold and liberal tastes only.

➕ C4 ✉ 1723 N. Halstead ☎ 312/867-0110 Ⓜ Brown Line: Armitage 🚌 8

BEN PAO ($$)

www.benpao.com
Inventive and inspired take on Chinese regional dishes, served under subdued lighting. "Hot pot" tables allow diners to cook their own noodles fondue-style.

➕ E8 ✉ 52 W. Illinois Street ☎ 312/222-1888 Ⓜ Red Line: Grand 🚌 36

BIG BOWL CAFÉ ($–$$)

www.bigbowl.com
Delectable Chinese noodle dishes and Thai curries served in big bowls.

➕ F6 ✉ 6 E. Cedar Street ☎ 312/640-8888 🕐 Dinner only Sun Ⓜ Brown Line: Chicago 🚌 37, 41

BIN 36 ($–$$$)

www.bin36.com
Convivial River North loft-cum-wine bar café pours dozens of selections by the glass and in wine "flights" or tasting portions paired to French-inflected American food and a 50-offering cheese bar. Seating ranges from café tables to stools at the zinc-topped bar.

➕ E9 ✉ 339 N. Dearborn

HOT DOGS

To a Chicagoan, a hot dog is not merely a frank in a bun. The true Chicago hot dog is a Viennese beef sausage smeared with ketchup, mustard, relish, onions and hot peppers to taste. Brightly lit hot-dog outlets are a feature of the city. Among them are Gold Coast Dogs

✉ 159 N Wabash Avenue, and other locations ☎ 312/917-1677 🕐 Breakfast, lunch, dinner. Closed Sat–Sun Ⓜ Red line: Grand 🚌 29, 36

Street ☎ 312/755-9463 Ⓜ Red Line: Grand 🚌 22

BRASSERIE JO ($$–$$$)

www.brasseriejo.com
The Alsace native chef cooks up French comfort food in a classic brasserie setting with tile floors, wall mirrors and waiters in long white aprons.

➕ E8 ✉ 59 W. Hubbard Street ☎ 312/595-0800 Ⓜ Red Line: Grand 🚌 22

CHARLIE TROTTER'S ($$$$)

www.charlietrotters.com
Chicago top toque Charlie Trotter prepares a unique eight-course $125 prix-fixe menu each night, drawing the finest ingredients from around the world and the foodies that appreciate them.

➕ C3 ✉ 816 W. Armitage Street ☎ 312/248-6228 Ⓜ Brown Line: Armitage 🚌 8

CLUB LUCKY ($–$$)

www.clubluckychicago.com
The Italian menu is long at this lively neighborhood supper club in Backtown, though the food takes second place to the socializing.

➕ A4 ✉ 1824 W. Wabansia Street ☎ 773/227-2308 🕐 Dinner only weekends Ⓜ Blue Line: Damon 🚌 7

THE DINING ROOM ($$$$)

This restaurant in the luxurious Ritz-Carlton Hotel offers matchless contemporary French cuisine

from the carte or as a fixed-price meal. Expect tuxedoed waiters; crystal chandeliers

🕂 F7 ✉ 160 E. Pearson Street ☎ 312/226-1000 🕐 Dinner only 🚇 Red Line: Chicago 🚌 125, 157

ED DEBEVIC'S SHORT ORDER DELUXE ($–$$)

www.eddebevics.com
Great burgers, sandwiches and milk shakes served to the sound of 1950s and 1960s music.

🕂 F8 ✉ 640 N. Wells Street ☎ 312/664-1707 🕐 Breakfast only weekends 🚇 Brown Line: Chicago 🚌 37, 41

FRONTERA GRILL/TOPOLOBAMPO ($$–$$$)

www.fronterakitchens.com
Chef Rick Bayless introduced the nation to regional Mexican food from his Frontera Grill hotspot in River North. Adjoining Topolobampo is the fine dining counterpart to Frontera's fiesta feel; two of the city's best restaurants.

🕂 E8 ✉ 445 N. Clark Street ☎ 312/661-1434 🕐 Closed Sun–Mon 🚇 Red Line: Grand 🚌 22

GENE & GEORGETTI ($$$)

www.geneandgeorgetti.com
Many feel that this steak house—complete with the men's-club decor, gruff waiters and deliciously thick cuts of meat—is the best in the city. Non-

carnivores beware though, there's scant choice to satisfy you.

🕂 E8 ✉ 500 N. Franklin Street ☎ 312/527-3718 🕐 Closed Sun 🚇 Brown, Purple Lines: Merchandise Mart 🚌 37

LAWRY'S THE PRIME RIB ($$–$$$)

The primest of prime rib—the only option on the dinner menu here—is accompanied by such traditional favorites as Yorkshire pudding, mashed potatoes and salad or an enormous baked potato.

🕂 F8 ✉ 100 E. Ontario Street ☎ 312/787-5000 🕐 Dinner only weekends 🚇 Red Line: Grand 🚌 125

MK ($$–$$$)

Understated chic in a former paint factory, which chef Michael Kornick has

---

CHICAGO PIZZA

The first deep-dish pizza was created in 1943 at Chicago's Pizzeria Uno. The thick but light crust and a generous smothering of tomato sauce and mozzarella cheese, combined with a variety of toppings, helped make the Chicago pizza a full meal in itself, unlike the thin-crusted New York version. Uno Chicago Grill is deservedly as popular as ever.

🕂 F8 ✉ 29 E. Ohio Street ☎ 312/321-1000 🚇 Red Line: Grand 🚌 36

turned into a venue for trendsetting concoctions, including lobster in many guises.

🕂 D7 ✉ 868 N. Franklin Street ☎ 312/482-9179 🚇 Brown Line: Chicago 🚌 66

MORTON'S OF CHICAGO ($$–$$$)

Chicago takes steak seriously, and this is one of the best places to eat it. Porterhouses grilled to perfection are the stock-in-trade.

🕂 E7 ✉ 1050 N. State Street ☎ 312/266-4820 🕐 Dinner only 🚇 Red Line: Chicago 🚌 36

SCOOZI! ($$)

A vivacious spot for inventive Italian fare, Scoozi! is huge and often crowded with a young group. Look out for the giant tomato over the door.

🕂 E7 ✉ 410 W. Huron Street ☎ 312/943-5900 🕐 Dinner only Sun 🚇 Brown Line: Chicago 🚌 37, 41

SPIAGGIA ($$$)

Steamed mussels in garlic and tomato broth is just one of the specialties of this celebrity favorite. The adjoining Spiaggia Café is less costly and less formal, and serves excellent pizza and pasta dishes.

🕂 E6 ✉ 980 N. Michigan Avenue ☎ 312/280-2750 🕐 Dinner only Sun 🚇 Red Line: Chicago 🚌 145, 146, 147, 151

RESTAURANTS

NORTH SIDE

Perhaps the city's most history-rich quarter, the South Side hosted the first mansions in Chicago and the 1983 World's Columbian Exposition, and later welcomed black immigrants from the south.

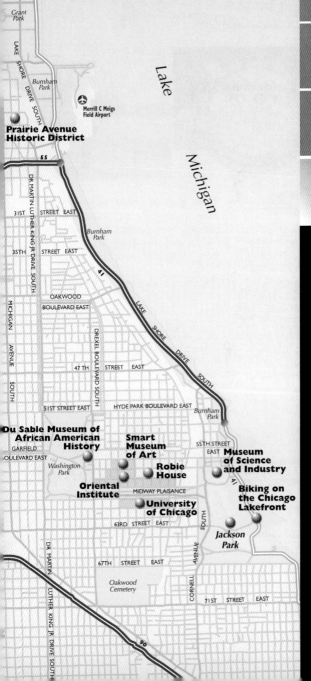

MONROE
STREET EAST

Grant
Park

LAKE SHORE DRIVE SOUTH

Burnham
Park

Lake

Merrill C Meigs
Field Airport

**Prairie Avenue
Historic District**

55

Michigan

DR MARTIN LUTHER KING JR DRIVE SOUTH

31ST   STREET   EAST

35TH   STREET   EAST

Burnham
Park

MICHIGAN AVENUE SOUTH

41

OAKWOOD
BOULEVARD EAST

DREXEL BOULEVARD SOUTH

LAKE SHORE DRIVE SOUTH

47 TH   STREET   EAST

51ST STREET EAST   HYDE PARK BOULEVARD EAST   Burnham
Park

**Du Sable Museum of
African American
History**

GARFIELD
BOULEVARD EAST

Washington
Park

**Smart
Museum
of Art**

**Robie
House**

55TH STREET
EAST   **Museum
of Science
and Industry**

**Oriental
Institute**

MIDWAY PLAISANCE

**University
of Chicago**

41   **Biking on
the Chicago
Lakefront**

63RD   STREET   EAST

SOUTH

CORNELL AVENUE

Jackson
Park

DR MARTIN LUTHER KING JR DRIVE SOUTH

67TH   STREET   EAST

Oakwood
Cemetery

71ST   STREET   EAST

90

Biking on the Chicago Lakefront

Bike tour and rental shop (left); following the lakefront (below)

THE BASICS

➕ Map page 83
✉ Chicago lakefront from Foster Beach on the north to 71st Street on the south
♿ Excellent
❓ Bike Chicago
✉ Navy Pier, 600 E. Grand Avenue ☎ 312/595-9600;
✉ 63rd Street Beach (63rd and Lake Shore Drive)
☎ 773/324-3400
💵 $10 per hour for a mountain bike or beach cruiser; $15 for a tandem and $25 for a quadcycle (four seater)

HIGHLIGHTS

● 18 miles (29km) of paved path
● 33 beaches
● Frequent concession stands in summer
● Views of the skyline
● Bike rentals

Some 18 miles (29km) of paved paths lures walkers, skaters and cyclists to the lakefront, combining exercise and sightseeing. The South Side offers busy busy routes and wonderful views.

Bike city Chicago is a particularly bike friendly city, counting over 100 miles (160km) of bike lanes and closing Lake Shore Drive for one day each summer so that cyclists can enjoy the route exclusively. Even the mayor is known to ride around the city streets on a two-wheeler. While the bike lanes on major urban thoroughfares scare the wits from out-of-towners, the lakefront bike path, free of auto traffic, enchants visitors as well as locals. North Side routes are popular and weekend crowds jam the lanes around Oak Street Beach where cyclists are forced to walk their bikes. For a quieter pedal, point your handlebars south and cruise past the Museum Campus down to the Museum of Science and Industry. The return trip lays out the entire skyline before you in photogenic panoramas as you pedal back. The level terrain is beginner-friendly.

Where to find wheels Bike Chicago offers several seasonal rental stands in Chicago. The best located for southbound trips are at Navy Pier or 63rd Street Beach. The "quadcycle," a four-seater vehicle only looks fun before you find you are pedaling for the entire family. Bike Chicago also offers city tours by bike each summer, two- to three-hour itineraries devoted to either Millennium Park, Lincoln Park or Grant Park.

African sculpture exhibit (below); exterior of the building (right)

DuSable Museum of African American History

One of Chicago's unsung museums, this one chronicles aspects of black history, chiefly focusing on African-Americans but also encompassing African and Caribbean cultures.

Settlers The museum is named after Chicago's first permanent settler, Jean-Baptiste Point du Sable, a Haitian trader born of a French father and African slave mother in whose home the city's first marriage, election and court decision occurred. Further African-American arrivals came in three main waves—during the late 19th century and during the two world wars—settling mostly on Chicago's South Side. Black businesses became established, while the expanding community provided the voter base for the first blacks to enter Chicago politics. Among the settlers were many musicians, and what became Chicago blues was born—an electrified urban form of rural blues fused with elements of jazz. The turbulent 1960s saw growing radicalism among Chicago's African-Americans, and the beginning of the rise to national prominence of South Side politician Jesse Jackson.

Exhibits The first-floor rooms display items from the permanent collection, including the Harold Washington Wing, which chronicles the triumph of Chicago's first black mayor in 1983. There are also meticulously planned temporary exhibitions, while the Arts and Crafts Festival, displaying original works on African-American themes, is held on the second weekend of July.

THE BASICS

www.dusablemuseum.org
✚ Map page 83
✉ 740 E. 56th Place
☎ 773/947-0600
🕐 Tue–Sat 10–5, Sun noon–5
🚇 Red Line: Garfield
🚌 59th Street
🚍 4
♿ Good
💲 Inexpensive; free on Sun

HIGHLIGHTS

● Slavery exhibit, including shackles
● African functional art, including stools and staffs
● Temporaty exhibits devoted to black music, art and history
● Craft fair
● Washington Park setting

Hitting a Blues Club

A performer and the audience at Blue Chicago

THE BASICS

Buddy Guy's Legends ▷ 35
New Checkerboard Lounge
▷ 93
Blue Chicago ▷ 76

HIGHLIGHTS

- Buddy Guy's Legends
- Blue Chicago
- New Checkerboard
Lounge
- Kingston Mines
- Rosa's Lounge

Southern blacks moving north in search of jobs in the 1940s amped up the acoustic blues in Chicago where hearing the music played live is one of the chief attractions of the city.

Blues background Blues music developed among African slaves working southern plantations and descended from "shout outs" of workers in the fields. By the 1920s it developed its signature musical style of repeated three-cord progressions. Vocalists center the genre, but performers regularly improvise solos above the musical background. Black America's mass exodus from the rural south to the urban north led many musicians to Chicago. The string bands of the Delta region borrowed from jazz groups in the city, amplifying the sound and adding drums, bass, piano and sometimes horns. Innovators Muddy Waters, B.B. King and Buddy Guy established Chicago's electric style, later widely copied by white players like Elvis Presley. The British rock invasion brought the Rolling Stones and Eric Clapton to town to jam with their blues heroes.

A city with the blues Since 1984, on the first weekend in June, marking the opening of summer, the city stages the Chicago Blues Festival, drawing 750,000 listeners to Grant Park. Admission is free and dedicated fest-goers come early with blankets and coolers to stake out their own place on the park lawn. The throng can get fairly boozy by evening, but is all-ages-recommended for most of its duration.

Clarke House exterior (below); main hall in the Glessner House (right)

Prairie Avenue District

After the city burned in the Great Fire of 1871, the wealthy and famous moved to the area around Prairie Avenue on the near South Side, where they built elegant mansions, some now open to tours.

From frontier to fancy Hostile Native Americans attacked European settlers in this district in what became known as the Fort Dearborn Massacre in 1812. Only after the Great Fire wiped out the city did builders reconsider the site. The who's who of Chicago society built here, including the Fields (of Field Museum fame), the Pullmans (responsible for luxury Pullman railroad cars) and the Armours (who made a fortune in meat-packing). Later generations would move north and build in the Gold Coast, leaving the Prairie Avenue District to decline. By the mid-20th century many were razed, arousing the passions of preservations who saved most of the 11 remaining Victorian mansions on roughly four blocks.

Two gems Much of the district provides eye candy for passersby, with the exception of two landmarked buildings open for tours.
 The oldest, the Greek Revival Clarke House originally owned by hardware dealer Henry B. Clarke, was actually moved to the area from a location farther south.
 The more unusual Glessner House is a stand-out in rugged granite with a fortresslike presence on a corner. The interior is considerably warmer, home to Arts and Crafts furnishings, a central courtyard and custom-made art.

THE BASICS

➕ F15
✉ 1800 and 1900-blocks of S. Prairie Avenue, 1800-block of S. Indiana, and 211-217 E. Cullerton Street

Glessner House Museum
www.glessnerhouse.org
Organizes guided tours of Clarke House also
✉ 1800 S. Prairie Avenue
☎ 312/326-1480
🕐 Tours Wed–Sun at 1, 2, 3 (reservations required)

Clarke House Museum
🕐 Tours Wed–Sun at 12, 1, 2 (reservations required)
🚇 Green, Orange, Red Lines: Roosevelt
🚌 1, 3, 4
♿ Fair
💵 Moderate; free on Wed

HIGHLIGHTS

● Clarke House
● Glessner House
● Self-guided strolls around the Victorian mansions

SOUTH SIDE

★ **TOP 25**

Museum of Science and Industry

HIGHLIGHTS

- U-505 submarine
- 1936 *Pioneer Zephyr* train
- The Chick Hatchery
- Miniature fairy castle
- Genetics exhibit
- Apollo 8 Command Module
- Omnimax Theater
- Walk-through heart

TIPS

- Ticket window line-ups are long. To avoid them, order your tickets in advance via the website and have them held at the will-call window.

With 35,000 artifacts spread across 14 acres (5.5ha), this museum easily fills a day. Even know-it-all visitors find hours passing like minutes as they discover new things about the world—and beyond—at every turn.

Flying high The first eye-catching item is a Boeing 727 attached to an interior balcony. Packed with multimedia exhibits, the plane simulates a flight from San Francisco to Chicago, making full use of flaps, rudders and undercarriage, all fully explained. Other flight-related exhibits include a simulated mission aboard a naval F-14 fighter. Reflecting other modes of transport are the 500mph (804kph) Spirit of America car, a walk-through 1944 German U-boat and the Apollo 8 spacecraft. The moon-circling Apollo craft forms

Clockwise from left: Robot exhibit; Pioneer Zephyr; children looking at a genetics exhibit; the U505 exhibit—the conning tower, a boy looks through the attack periscope, a demonstration in the control room

just a small part of the excellent Henry Crown Space Center, housed in an adjoining building.

Medical matters A walk-through heart sits among exhibits detailing the workings of the human body. Close by, in the AIDS exhibit, imaginative devices explain much about viruses and the workings of the immune system. The display has a computer-generated voyage into the body, which illustrates the attack strategy of the HIV virus and the approaches used by scientists to combat it.

Industrial issues Addressing industry, MSI recreates a coal mine, complete with a simulated descent to 600 feet (180m) below the earth's surface to the coal seam in miner's cars. The Farm exhibit allows visitors to climb into a John Deere combine and virtually harvest a corn field.

THE BASICS

www.msichicago.org
🕂 Map page 83
✉ 57th Street at Lake Shore Drive
☎ 312/684-1414
🕒 Summer: daily 9.30–5.30; rest of the year: hours vary, call for times
🍴 Several cafés
🚇 Red Line: Garfield
🚌 55th, 56th, 57th street
🚍 6, 10
♿ Excellent
💲 Moderate; free on Thu; separate charge for Omnimax Theater

More to See

CHINATOWN
The ornate Chinatown Gate arching over Cermak at Wentworth marks the center of Chinatown, the dense pocket of some eight blocks surrounding the intersection. The oldest Chinese district in the city was founded by 19th-century railroad workers.

🚩 D15 🚇 Red Line: Cermak/Chinatown 🚌 24

JACKSON PARK
In 1893, 27 million people attended the World's Columbian Exposition, in what became Jackson Park, now a green space with sports courts, a Japanese garden and the Museum of Science and Industry (▷ 88).

🚩 Map page 83 ✉ Between S. Stony Island Avenue and Lake Michigan 🚇 Red Line: Garfield 🚌 55th, 56th, 57th streets 🚌 6, 10

JANE ADDAMS HULL-HOUSE MUSEUM
www.uic.edu/jaddams/hull/hull_house.html
An impoverished immigrant's grim lot was made less miserable by the work of Jane Addams. In the late 19th-century she created Hull House, a center in one of the city's neediest neighborhoods. Hull House offered English-language and US citizenship courses, child care and other services. A 15-minute slide show tells the story. The rooms of the main building are lined by furnishings and memorabilia including letters, photos, awards and books from the house library.

🚩 C11 ✉ 800 S. Halsted Street ☎ 312/413-5353 🕐 Tue–Fri 10–4, Sun noon–5 🚇 Blue Line: UIC-Halsted 🚌 Halsted 🚌 8 ♿ Fair 🎟 Free

MEXICAN FINE ARTS CENTER MUSEUM
www.mfacmchicago.org
Explore Mexican culture through this collection of some 5,000 works by artists of Mexican nationality or descent. Exhibits include prints and drawings, photography, contemporary paintings and sculpture.

🚩 Map page 83 ✉ 1852 W. 19th Street ☎ 312/738-1503 🕐 Tue–Sun 10–5 🚇 Blue Line: 18th Street 🚌 18 ♿ Good

Japanese Gardens in Jackson Park

ORIENTAL INSTITUTE

www.oi.uchicago.edu
The University of Chicago's Oriental Institute is a leading museum and research center specializing in the Middle East. Amid the mummy masks and royal seals, sizeable pieces stand out. Dominating the Egyptian section is a statue of Tutankhamun. In the Assyrian section is the human-headed winged bull from the palace of Sargon II (*R*.721–705BC).

🗺 Map page 83 ✉ 1155 E. 58th Street ☎ 312/702-9520 🕐 Tue, Thu–Sat 10–6, Wed 10–8.30, Sun noon–6 Ⓡ Red Line: Garfield 🚉 59th Street 🚌 4, 55 ♿ Good ✋ Inexpensive

ROBIE HOUSE (1910)

A famed example of Frank Lloyd Wright's Prairie School style of architecture. The horizontal emphasis reflects the Midwest's open spaces.

🗺 Map page 83 ✉ 5757 S. Woodlawn Avenue ☎ 708/848-1976 🕐 Guided tours: Mon–Fri 11, 1, 3. Continuous tours: Sat–Sun 11–3.30 Ⓖ Green Line: Cottage Grove 🚉 59th Street 🚌 4 ♿ Few ✋ Free

SMART MUSEUM OF ART

www.smartmuseum.uchicago.edu
The museum holds over 10,000 objects. The only museum of its kind on the South Side is a hidden gem and is strong in postwar Chicago art, Japanese painting and contemporary Chinese photography.

🗺 Map page 83 ✉ 5550 S. Greenwood Avenue ☎ 773/702-0200 🕐 Tue, Wed, Fri 10–4, Thu 10–8, Sat–Sun 11–5 Ⓖ Green Line: Garfield 🚌 55

UNIVERSITY OF CHICAGO

www.uchicago.edu
The oldest buildings on the leafy campus are in English Gothic style, but modernists Eero Saarinen and Ludwig Mies van der Rohe added boxier structures in the 1950s and '60s. Guided tours are offered primarily to prospective students, though the campus makes a nice spot for a stroll if you're in the area.

🗺 Map page 83 ✉ Campus is largely bounded by Blackstone Avenue, Cottage Grove, 55th Street and 59th Street Ⓖ Green Line: Garfield 🚌 55, 170, 171, 172

Interior of the Smart Museum (above)

A relief on the exterior of the Oriental Institute (right)

South Side Shuffle

The best place for a walk on the South Side is between Lake Michigan and the University of Chicago.

DISTANCE: Approximately 2.5 miles (4km) **ALLOW:** 2 hours

START

MUSEUM OF SCIENCE AND INDUSTRY
(▷ 88) 🚇 Green Line: Garfield 🚌 6, 10, 15, 55

END

WOODLAWN TAP (▷ 93)
🚇 Red, Green Lines: Garfield 🚌 55

1 Begin with a look at the Museum of Science and Industry. The place is so vast it could easily take your whole day.

8 Walk north on Ellis Avenue three blocks until you reach 55th Street. Take a right and continue to the Woodlawn Tap for refreshments.

2 Exit the museum on the south side facing the Jackson Park Lagoon, created by New York's famed Central Park designer Frederick Law Olmsted for the world's fair.

7 Walk one block west on 58th Street, passing the artifact-rich Oriental Institute, to reach the main quadrangle of the campus and admire the Gothic-inspired Cobb Hall and Bond Chapel.

3 Loop the shore on the east side of the Lagoon until you are opposite the museum where North Bridge leads to Wooded Island and the lovely restored Osaka Japanese Garden.

6 Continue north on Woodlawn one block to admire the Robie House designed by Frank Lloyd Wright and open for tours.

4 Leave Jackson Park heading west along Midway Plaisance, between Jackson Park and the western division now known as Washington Park.

5 At Woodlawn and 59t Street just opposite the Midway, pop into the Rockefeller Memorial Chapel.

WALK

SOUTH SIDE

BABY DOLL POLKA CLUB

Some come for the kitsch, others for the oom-pah beat, but both audiences head across the street from Midway Airport for the city's only all-polka bar with live music and dancing.
- ✉ 6102 S. Central Avenue
- ☎ 773/582-9706
- Ⓜ Orange Line: Midway Airport 🚌 63

COURT THEATRE

www.courttheatre.org
The University of Chicago's theater has been staging high-quality dramas and musicals for more than 50 years. Noted for its fine acting and innovative staging, the Court deserves the attention more easily snared by downtown and North Side troops.
- ✉ 5535 W. Ellis Avenue
- ☎ 773/753-4472
- Ⓜ Green Line: Garfield
- 🚌 55

DRU'S

Tucked away in Chinatown is this stylish bar-cum-club-cum-eatery, with a well-stocked bar and a hip clientele.
- ✉ 2101 S. China Place
- ☎ 312/567-9349 Ⓜ Red Line: Cermak/Chinatown
- 🚌 24

NEW CHECKERBOARD LOUNGE FOR BLUES 'N' JAZZ

The fabled Checkerboard Lounge, a longtime South Side blues club on 43rd Street, staged shows by the likes of Muddy Waters. The club closed in 2003 only to reopen in Hyde Park, close to the University of Chicago where music fans again come to get the blues.
- ✉ 5201 S. Harper Avenue
- ☎ 773/684-1472
- Ⓜ Green Line: 51st 🚌 28

OMNIMAX THEATER

www.msichicago.org
A curving, five-story screen embedded with 72 speakers shows large-format IMAX movies on subjects both scientific and entertaining in a separate building attached to the Museum of Science and Industry.
- ✉ 57th Street and Lake Shore Drive ☎ 773/684-1414
- Ⓜ Green Line: Garfield
- 🚌 6, 10, 15, 55

CHINESE NEW YEAR

At the end of January thousands of visitors flock to Chinatown to celebrate Chinese New Year. The parade features dragon dancers, martial artists and Chinese dancers as well as the incongruous bagpipe marching band and assorted politicians. The route runs through the heart of the neighborhood on Wentworth from Cermak to 24th Street. Afterwards parade-goers jam the many area restaurants for dim sum.

VELVET LOUNGE

www.velvetlounge.net
Chicago saxophonist Fred Anderson runs one of the city's most revered jazz listening rooms. The original was destroyed to make way for housing but the club survived the move, with the city's best players on the calendar.
- ✉ 67 E. Cermak Road
- ☎ 312/791-9050
- Ⓜ Red Line: Cermak
- 🚌 21, 29

WOODLAWN TAP

Chicago is famed for its neighborhood taverns, corner taps that serve as places where communities bind. Hyde Park lacks the saloons of other neighborhoods, but the Woodlawn Tap, also known as "Jimmy's," goes a long way to fill in, with three dim rooms filled with brainy academics deep in conversation.
- ✉ 1172 E. 55th Street
- ☎ 773/643-5516
- Ⓜ Red, Green Lines: Garfield
- 🚌 55

Restauants

PRICES

Prices are approximate, based on a 3-course meal for one person.

$$$$	over $50
$$$	$31–$50
$$	$16–$30
$	up to $15

EMPEROR'S CHOICE ($$–$$$)

At this small, intimate restaurant, portraits of former Chinese emperors hang above diners feasting on some of Chinatown's most creative seafood dishes. For a special occasion order Peking duck a day in advance.

✉ 2238 S. Wentworth Avenue
☎ 312/225-8800 🚇 Red Line: Cermak/Chinatown
🚌 24

GIOCO ($$–$$$)

www.kdkrestaurants.com
Fine Tuscan and Umbrian menu combining pizzas, homemade pastas and roast meats served in a former speakeasy.

✉ 1312 S. Wabash Avenue
☎ 312/939-3870
🎭 Dinner only 🚇 Red, Orange, Green Lines: Roosevelt 🚌 4

HEALTHY FOOD LITHUANIAN RESTAURANT ($)

Beneath the Lithuanian scenes that decorate the walls, this spartan South Side spot serves dishes from the Baltic country, including mushroom barley soup and homemade sausages.

✉ 3226 S. Halsted Street
☎ 312/326–3724 🚇 Orange Line: Halsted 🚌 8

LA PETITE FOLIE ($$–$$$)

A rare, fine-dining outpost in Hyde Park, La Petite Folie serves unfussy French food. This is a popular pre-curtain spot for Court Theatre patrons.

✉ 1504 E. 55th Street
☎ 773/493-1394 🎭 No lunch weekends. Closed Mon 🚇 Green Line: Garfield 🚌 55

PHOENIX ($$)

Popular Chinatown restaurants serves up panoramic views of the Chicago skyline from picture windows, along with a lively dim sum trade in which servers wheel around small dishes of dumplings, barbecue and meat-filled buns and diners orders. Many waiters do not speak good English; good humor and the pointing method of ordering prevail. Long waits are common on weekends.

✉ 2131 S. Archer Avenue
☎ 312/328-0848
🚇 Red Line: Cermak
🚌 21, 24

OPERA ($$$)

www.opera-chicago.com
Theatrical decor in a former Paramount film warehouse, Opera features upscaled Asian dishes with bold flavors like five-spice squid and Cantonese lobster. Creative cocktails fuel the people-watching in this bustling hotspot

✉ 1301 S. Wabash Avenue
☎ 312/461-0161
🎭 Dinner only 🚇 Red, Orange, Green Lines: Roosevelt 🚌 4

ZAPATISTA ($–$$)

www.zapatistacantina.com
Lively Mexican outpost Zapatista combines regional Mexican dishes such as Oaxacan *moles* and Yucatecan *ceviches* in one eager-to-please menu. The drinks list, too, is comprehensive.

✉ 1307 S. Wabash Avenue
☎ 312/435-1307
🚇 Red, Orange, Green Lines: Roosevelt 🚌 4

CHICAGO'S LITTLE ITALY

Taylor Street was the heart of the immigrant Italian community nearly a century ago. A few old-timers still live in the district but the Italian restaurant scene thrives along a few blocks of Taylor. Rosebud Café (1500 W. Taylor Street) jams fans in for pastas and a convivial atmosphere. Francesca's on Taylor (1400 W. Taylor Street) does homemade pastas in an urban-chic room. The casual Pompei Bakery (1531 W. Taylor Street) serves the best pizza by the slice on the street.

Ironically one of the top tourist sights isn't even in the city. Frank Lloyd Wright's home and original office is in Oak Park. Some 198 neighborhoods aim to lure you, particularly Wicker Park and Bucktown.

WESTERN

Loyola University,
Lake Shore

Lake

14

ASHLAND

AVENUE

41

NORTH

AVE NUE

Lincoln
Park

Montrose
Harbor

*Graceland
Cemetery*

WEST

Michigan

ING PARK ROAD

NORTH

Belmont
Harbor

**Wrigley Field
Stadium**

41

**Boys
Town**

North
Pond

Chicago River North Branch

94

Diversey
Harbor

Lincoln
Park

cker Park
**Boutique
Browsing**

South
Pond

**OLD
TOWN**

CHICAGO

olish Museum
of America

Chicago River

Union Park

LOOP

Grant
Park

Buckingham Fountain

John G Shedd Aquarium

Adler Planetarium

ROOSEVELT ROAD WEST

**Field Museum of
Natural History**

Burnham Park
Harbor

HALSTED

55

Arnold Canal

LAKE

WESTERN

STREET

McKinley
Park

ASHLAND

90

94

MICHIGAN

SHORE

DRIVE

41

WEST

SOUTH

BOULEVARD

AVENUE

47TH

AVENUE STREET

SOUTH

**Museum of
Science and
Industry**

Sherman
Park

SOUTH

GARFIELD BOULEVARD

Washington
Park

WEST

ge
rk

63RD STREET WEST

**University
of Chicago**

East
Lagoon

Ogden
Park

90

Jackson
Park

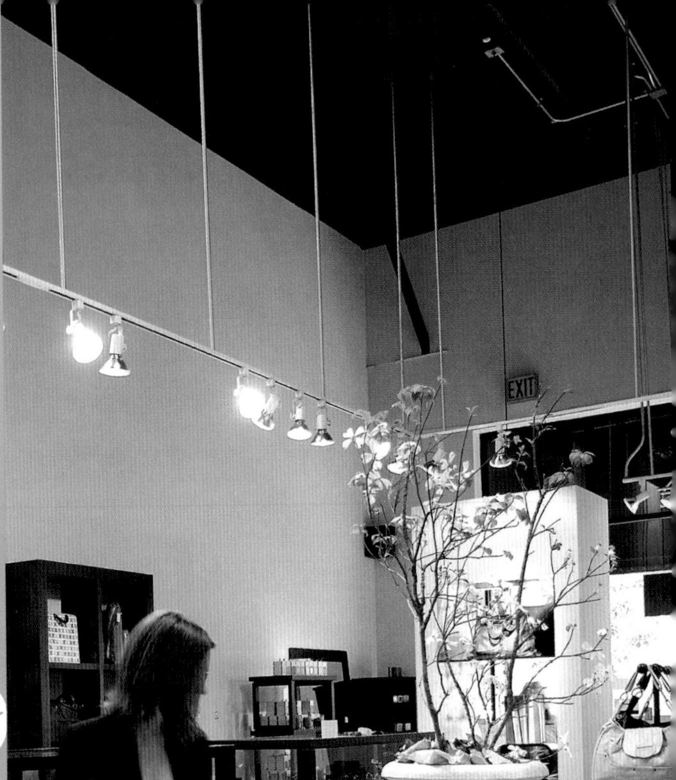
EXIT

Interiors of Stitch (left), P45 (below), City Soles (right)

Boutique Browsing in Wicker Park/Bucktown

Roughly 2 miles (3km) due west of the Gold Coast following North Avenue, the scene changes entirely. The urban neighborhood mixes artists, yuppies, immigrants and some of the best shopping and nightlife in the city.

History In the mid-1850s Irish immigrants settled in around the Rolling Mill Steel Works. Businesses lined the commercial avenues and residences are tucked in tree-shaded streets behind them. After the Great Fire of 1871 the area boomed as the well-heeled built spacious Victorian mansions. Waves of immigrant Germans, Norwegians, Jews and Poles worked their way through the area following Milwaukee Avenue out of downtown. From 1930s to the 1970s the area declined. From the 1980s the neighborhoods—Wicker Park to the south and Bucktown adjacent north—took off as trendy nightclubs, restaurants and shops moved in.

Where to shop There is so much choice here. Embelezar (1639 N. Damen Avenue) sells lush looks for the home, neighbored by P45 (1643 N. Damen Avenue) selling cutting-edge women's clothing from emerging American designers, and Helen Yi (1645 N. Damen Avenue) with streamlined apparel for women. Pagoda Red (1714 N. Damen Avenue) imports antiques from Asia ranging from massive Chinese cabinets to fans. Stitch (1723 N. Damen Avenuye) is the place for accessories, City Soles (2001 North Avenue) for shoes and Scoop NYC (1702 N. Milwaukee Avenue) for trendy casual clothes.

THE BASICS

www.
wickerparkbucktown.com
⊞ Map page 97
⊠ The center of the neighborhood is at the three-way intersection of Milwaukee, Damen and North avenues.
🕐 Most shops Mon–Sat 11–7, Sun 12–5
🚇 Blue Line: Damen
🚌 50, 72

HIGHLIGHTS

● P45
● Helen Yi
● Embelezar
● Pagoda Red
● Stitch
● City Soles

FARTHER AFIELD

TOP 25

Frank Lloyd Wright
Home and Studio

TOP 25

- Barrel-vaulted playroom
- Drafting Room with chain harness system to support the roof
- Stained-glass leaded windows
- Skylights
- Wright-designed furniture

TIPS

- Advanced tickets are highly recommended. Get them up to midnight the night before the tour from the website. You cannot order by phone.

The Frank Lloyd Wright's Home and Studio provides an insight into the early ideas of one of the greatest and most influential architects of the 20th century. It is an essential stop for anyone interested in design, or in the ability of one man to realize his extraordinary vision.

Organic ideas Working for the Chicago architect Louis Sullivan, the 22-year-old Frank Lloyd Wright designed this home in 1889 for himself, his first wife and their children, and furnished it with pieces he designed. The shingled exterior is not typical of Wright, but the bold geometric shape stands out among the neighboring Queen Anne-style houses. Inside, the open plan, central fireplaces and low ceilings are the earliest examples of the elements that became fundamental in

The exterior of Frank Lloyd Wright's Home (left); the Children's Playroom inside the house

Wright's so-called Prairie School of Architecture. Particularly notable are the children's playroom, the high-backed chairs in the dining room and the willow tree that grows through the walls in keeping with Wright's theory of organic architecture—architecture in harmony with its surroundings.

Prairie views In 1893, Wright opened his own practice in an annex to the house: a concealed entrance leads into an office showcasing many of Wright's ideas, such as suspended lamps and an open-plan work space. The draftsmen once employed here on seminal Prairie School buildings worked in a stunningly designed room in sight of what was then open prairie. Lloyd Wright's disciples designed 125 buildings here, including the nearby Unity Temple and the Robie House in Hyde Park on Chicago's South Side.

THE BASICS

www.wrightplus.org
✚ Map page 96
✉ 951 Chicago Avenue, Oak Park
☎ 708/848-1976
🕐 Guided tours only: Mon–Fri 11, 1, 3; Sat–Sun 11–3.30 every 20 mins
🚇 Green Line: Oak Park Avenue
🚆 Oak Park
🚌 23
♿ Few
⚑ Moderate

More to See

BALZEKAS MUSEUM OF LITHUANIAN CULTURE

Regional folk costumes and other Lithuanian historical items form part of an extensive and absorbing collection.

✉ 6500 S. Pulaski Road ☎ 773/582-6500 🕐 Daily 10–4 🚇 Orange Line: Midway 🚌 53A ♿ Few 💵 Inexpensive

ERNEST HEMINGWAY MUSEUM

www.ehfop.org

A collection remembering the Nobel Prize-winning writer who spent his first 18 years in Oak Park. Open the same hours at No. 339 North, is Hemingway's birthplace.

✉ 200 N. Oak Park Avenue ☎ 708/848–2222 🕐 Mon–Fri, Sun 1–5, Sat 10–5 🚇 Green Line: Harlem 🚉 Oak Park 🚌 23 ♿ Few 💵 Moderate

FRANK LLOYD WRIGHT TOUR

www.wrightplus.org

The Oak Park neighborhood surrounding the architect's home and studio hosts 26 Wright-designed homes, the largest concentration of Wright buildings anywhere in the world. The Wright Foundation rents headsets for self-guided walks past the private homes on routes that last about one hour. Take the tour after visiting the Frank Lloyd Wright Home and Studio, which will familiarize you with the Prairie School style.

✉ Oak Park ☎ 708/848-1976 🚇 Green Line: Oak Park Avenue 🚌 23 ♿ Few 💵 Moderate

GARFIELD PARK CONSERVATORY

www.garfield-conservatory.org

Providing a refuge from the city, the conservatory has 5 acres (2ha) of tropical and subtropical plants, and is open daily, all year round. The highlights include extensive collections of palms, ferns and cacti. Chicagoans come here for expert gardening tips and for shows, when the opening hours are extended.

🗺 Map page 96 ☎ 773/638-1766 🕐 Sun–Wed, Fri–Sat 9–5, Thu 9–8 🚇 Green Line: Conservatory-Central Park 🚌 82 ♿ Few 💵 Free

Detail of a mural at the Lithuanian Village (above)

Walter H. Gale's House, designed by Frank Lloyd Wright (right)

Shopping

57TH STREET BOOKS

A Hyde Park institution, with new and used volumes. Toys are provided for children of browsing parents.

✉ 1301 E. 57th Street
☎ 773/684-1300
Ⓜ Red Line: Garfield
🚌 55th, 56th, 57th Street
🚌 1, 4, 28, 51

THE ALLEY

www.thealley.com
If your idea of an accessory is a Zippo lighter or a Che Guevara belt buckle, the Alley stores, a group of alternative clothing stockists, is just the place to find it, plus leather jackets and motorcycle boots.

✉ 3228 N. Clark Street
☎ 773/883-1800
Ⓜ Brown or Red Lines: Belmont 🚌 22, 36

BEATNIX

Packed from floor to ceiling, this stash of wild and unbelievable attire is Disneyland for the daring.

✉ 3400 N. Halsted Avenue
☎ 773/281-6933
Ⓜ Brown, Red Lines: Belmont
🚌 152

BELMONT ARMY SURPLUS

This former army surplus store has expanded over three floors to become a top Chicago spot for hiking boots, backpacks and more.

✉ 945 W. Belmont Avenue
☎ 773/549-1038
Ⓜ Brown, Red Lines: Belmont
🚌 77

BROADWAY ANTIQUES MARKET

www.bamchicago.com
The 75-plus dealers at this two-floor antiques haven sell everything from art deco to mid-20th-century modern.

✉ 6130 N. Broadway Avenue
☎ 773/743-5444 Ⓜ Red Line: Granville 🚌 136

DSW SHOE WAREHOUSE

www.dswshoe.com
Whether in need of designer shoes for a top night out or simply solid footwear, this long established outlet is the place to find them.

✉ 3131 N. Clark Street
☎ 773/975-7182 Ⓜ Brown, Red Lines: Belmont 🚌 77

SPORTSWORLD

Appropriately neighboring Wrigley Field, this stocks the biggest array of Chicago Cubs clothing imaginable, plus wearable

---

CURIOUS CLOTHES

Should the sensible buying of sensible clothes for sensible everyday wear suddenly become a stultifyingly dull pursuit, you can let your sartorial imaginations run riot at Chicago Costume Company (✉ 1120 W. Fullerton Parkway). This enormous store carries hundreds of outrageous costumes, masks and assorted outlandish accessories for sale or rent, for the dresser who dares.

---

souvenirs of Wrigley Field itself.

✉ 1027 W. Addison Street
☎ 773/472-7701 Ⓜ Red Line: Addison
🚌 22, 152

UNABRIDGED BOOKSTORE

Chicago's leading gay bookstore and a rare independent bookseller offers reads on a wide array of topics. Well-read employees offer their personal touts for books they like in notes attached to the racks.

✉ 3251 N. Broadway
☎ 773/883-9119
Ⓜ Red Line: Belmont
🚌 36, 77

UNCLE FUN

www.unclefunchicago.com
All ages from elementary schoolkids to their parents love to browse Uncle Fun, crammed with vintage metal wind-up toys, cast-off stickers, cheap plastic animals, gag gifts and trinkets. Uncle Fun's owners also run the stationery shop Paper Boy across the street with considerably more serious, artistically inclined cards, gift wrap and pens.

✉ 1338 W. Belmont Street
☎ 773/477-8223
Ⓜ Brown Line: Paulina
🚌 77

Entertainment and Nightlife

BEAT KITCHEN

Smallish venue that makes a good setting for folk and rock acts, predominantly from around Chicago.

✉ 2100 W. Belmont Avenue
☎ 773/281-4444
Ⓣ Brown, Red Lines: Belmont
🚌 22

CHICAGO CENTER FOR THE PERFORMING ARTS

An expanding and well-equipped performance art and education complex staging diverse drama and music in its 350-seat main hall, as well as other events.

✉ 777 N. Green Street
☎ 312/327-2000
Ⓣ Blue Line: Chicago
🚌 8, 66

CHICAGO THEATER COMPANY

This African-American company stages some of the city's best contemporary productions at theaters around town. The repertoire mixes original material with adaptations.

✉ 500 E. 67th Street
☎ 773/493-0901 🚌 3

CUBBY BEAR LOUNGE

Its location opposite Wrigley Field makes this sports bar a favorite spot for post-Cub games. Live music spans rock, country, reggae and blues. Dancing and beer.

✉ 1059 W. Addison Street
☎ 773/327-1662 Ⓣ Brown Lne: Addison 🚌 22, 152

ELBO ROOM

Innovative venue for live alternative rock, poetry readings and comedy.

✉ 2871 N. Lincoln Avenue
☎ 773/549–5549 Ⓣ Brown Line: Diversey 🚌 11

GREEN MILL COCKTAIL LOUNGE

www.greenmilljazz.com
Classic Uptown jazz club dates back to Chicago's Prohibition Days as a speakeasy. Home of the Sunday night Uptown Poetry Slam, an open mike night for performance poets that has spawned imitators the world over.

✉ 4802 N. Broadway Avenue
☎ 773/878-5552 Ⓣ Red Line: Lawrence 🚌 36

METRO

Major mid-size venue for live rock, with ample space for dancing and

RAVINIA FESTIVAL
From mid-June to Labor Day, the northern suburb of Highland Park plays host to the Ravinia Festival. The summer home of the Chicago Symphony Orchestra, Ravinia also stages rock and jazz concerts, dance events and other cultural activities. Chartered buses ferry festival goers the 25 miles (40km) from central Chicago; you can also get there by commuter train. Details ☎ 847/433–8819; www.ravinia.org.

plentiful seating with good views. Other levels have a nightclub and coffee bar.

✉ 3730 N. Clark Street
☎ 773/549- 0203 Ⓣ Brown Line: Addison 🚌 22, 152

MUSIC BOX THEATRE

www.musicboxtheatre.com
Independent, classic and foreign films fill the slate at this 1929 Lakeview movie palace with twinkling stars in the ceiling and an organ employed during Christmas holiday sing-alongs.

✉ 3733 N. Southport Avenue
☎ 773/871-6604 Ⓣ Brown Line: Southport 🚌 9, 77, 80

SHEFFIELD'S WINE & BEER

On a sunny day, head for the patio bar to sample the selection of microbrews, most made on the premises.

✉ 3258 N. Sheffield Avenue
☎ 773/281-4989 Ⓣ Brown, Red Lines: Belmont 🚌 9, 77

THE WILD HARE

Top-notch live reggae and other Caribbean and African sounds in the heart of Wrigleyville.

✉ 3530 N. Clark Street
☎ 773/327-4273 Ⓣ Brown Line: Addison 🚌 22, 152

Restaurants

PRICES

Prices are approximate, based on a 3-course meal for one person.

$$$$	over $50
$$$	$31–$50
$$	$16–$30
$	up to $15

ARUN'S ($$$$)

Superb Thai fare, with subtle spicing reflecting the exceptional talent in the kitchen. Tasting menus only.

✉ 4156 N. Kedzie Avenue ☎ 773/539-1909 ⊙ Dinner only. Closed Mon 🚇 Brown Line: Kedzie 🚌 80, 82

BARBAKAN RESTAURANT ($)

Unprepossessing interior, complete with ageing formica tables, conceals delicious Polish food at low prices; the soup options change daily.

✉ 3308 N. Milwaukee Avenue ☎ 773/202-8181 🚇 Blue Line: Belmont 🚌 85

BISTRO CAMPAGNE ($$$)

www.bistrocampagne.com Intimate setting for quality French cuisine from a small but well-chosen menu; come early in the week to avoid a crowded scene. Outdoor dining in summer in a pleasant garden.

✉ 4518 N. Lincoln Avenue ☎ 773/271-6100 ⊙ Dinner only; Sun brunch 🚇 Brown Line: Western 🚌 11, 49, 78

CAFÉ LURA ($)

Live music and cabaret provides reason to call here in the evenings, but stop in earlier in the day for the Polish fare.

✉ 3184 N. Milwaukee Avenue ☎ 773/736-3033 🚇 Blue Line: Belmont 🚌 56, 77

CHICAGO BRAUHAUS ($$–$$$)

www.chicagobrauhaus.com Chicago has lost many of its famed German restaurants. The 40-plus-year-old Brauhaus proudly waves the flag with a menu of plentiful standards like schnitzel and sausage and frothy beers on tap. The house oompah band gets dancers to their feet.

✉ 4732 N. Lincoln Avenue ☎ 773/784-4444 ⊙ No lunch Sat. Closed Tue 🚇 Brown Line: Western 🚌 11, 4

INDIA IN CHICAGO

Chicago's Indian community thrives along Devon Avenue on the far North Side of the city. Bollywood video stores and sari shops occasionally intersperse the long string of restaurants that line either side of the street west of Western Avenue. Top choices include Moti Maha (2525 W. Devon Avenue), Indian Garden (2546 W. Devon Avenue) and Tiffin (2536 W. Devon Avenue). Many places feature a bargain-price buffet for the midday meal.

JOY'S NOODLE AND RICE ($)

Great-value Thai dishes served without fuss; portions are modest.

✉ 3257 N. Broadway ☎ 773/327-8330 🚇 Brown, Red Lines: Belmont 🚌 36, 77

MIA FRANCESCA ($$)

www.miafrancesca.com There is always a wait at this favorite of Chicago natives. Excellent seafood specials and wonderful red-sauced fare, but it's the pasta in large amounts and top-notch pizza that make this undersized eatery one of Lake View's most popular.

✉ 3311 N. Clark Street ☎ 773/281-3310 ⊙ Lunch only Sat–Sun 🚇 Brown, Red, Purple Lines: Belmont 🚌 22, 77

SPRING ($$–$$$)

www.springrestaurant.net A downtown-caliber restaurant in Wicker Park, Spring specializes in Asian-inflected seafood dishes prepared with high quality ingredients and plated elegantly. The semi-underground digs were once a Russian bathhouse bearing the original glazed white tiles.

✉ 2039 W. North Avenue ☎ 773/395-7100 ⊙ Dinner only. Closed Mon 🚇 Blue Line: Damen 🚌 50, 72

Where to Stay

Chicago's hotels are largely clustered downtown within walking distance of shopping, restaurants, nightlife and museums. Around O'Hare Airport are lodgings that cater primarily to business travelers.

Introduction

Chicago's hotels concentrate in the tourist regions downtown. But within that region, where you stay depends very much on what you aim to do.

An Experience
If it's shopping you seek, look for something on the near North Side or along the Magnificent Mile. Loop district hotels plant you closest to many top cultural attractions, including the Art Institute of Chicago and Randolph Street theaters. River North hotels provide great access to restaurants and nightlife. To experience life as a Chicago resident you might try something in close proximity to Wrigley Field or the Lincoln Park Zoo.

For Your Own Budget
Most of the city's luxury hotels, including the Peninsula, Ritz-Carlton and Four Seasons, are on or around the Magnificent Mile, offering easy access to high-end shops. Mid-range hotels are scattered throughout the Loop, River North and near North Side regions. Budget hotels tend to be pushed to the margins of downtown or in North Side neighborhoods such as Lakeview.

Best Times to Visit
Because business travel traffic is so vital to hoteliers, many of them drop their rates to lure in weekend guests. You likely will not find such bargains in the height of summer, but during the off-season the sales can be dramatic.

DATES TO AVOID
Chicago has the biggest convention center in the country, McCormick Place. Some conventions swell to take every hotel room in the region. Others, such as the national restaurant show each May, make getting a restaurant reservation difficult. Business travelers account for 55 percent of hotel business downtown. September, October, November and May are big convention months. If crowds concern you, phone ahead when booking your hotel and ask about group business during your stay.

Budget Hotels

PRICES

Expect to pay between $75 and $150 for a budget hotel.

BEST WESTERN HAWTHORNE TERRACE

www.hawthorneterrace.com
Wrigley Field is a short walk from this 55-room neighborhood inn with nice-for-the-price amenities including Wi-Fi and a fitness center. Also close to Wrigleyville and North Halsted restaurant scene, as well as the Lincoln Park lakefront.

➕ Off map at C1 ✉ 3434 N. Broadway ☎ 888/860-3400; fax 773/244-3435 🚇 Red Line: Addison 🚌 36

CASS HOTEL

www.casshotel.com
Once past the forlorn lobby and the shabby downstairs bar you will find 180 clean rooms at a budget price within easy reach of the Magnificent Mile and River North. Also has free Wi-Fi internet access in its café and (paid for) internet access from a public kiosk in the lobby area.

➕ F8 ✉ 640 N. Wabash Avenue ☎ 800/227-7850 or 312/787-4030; fax 312/787-8544 🚇 Red Line: Grand 🚌 29, 65

DAYS INN LINCOLN PARK NORTH

www.lpndaysinn.com
A 133-room motel at the busy intersection of Broadway, Clark and Diversey, and walking distance to Wrigley Field. Price includes continental breakfast buffet. Free Wi-Fi.

➕ Off map at D1 ✉ 644 W. Diversey Parkway ☎ 773/525-7010 or 888/576-3297; fax 773/525-6998 🚇 Brown Line: Diversey 🚌 22

HOSTEL CHICAGO INTERNATIONAL

www.hichicago.org
Also known as the J. Ira & Nicki Harris Family Hostel, this 1886 building on the southern edge of the Loop offers comfortable beds in 500 immaculate if spartan dorms that provide a perfect low-budget stay. Guests qualify for a range of discounts on local tours and other attractions.

➕ F11 ✉ 24 E. Congress Parkway ☎ 312/360-0300 🚇 Red Line: Harrison 🚌 6, 146

B&BS

Bed-and-breakfasts are typically Victorian homes fitted out in sumptuous style and filled with antiques. They span all price categories and there is a particularly strong concentration in Oak Park. The Bed & Breakfast Chicago agency (☎ 800/375-7084; www.athomeinchicago.com) operates a reservation system; it handles properties that are usually centrally located.

OHIO HOUSE

This dependable, simple motel has 50 rooms and offers exceptional rates in a River North location. Adjoining coffee shop.

➕ E8 ✉ 600 N. La Salle Street ☎ 312/943-6000; fax 312/943-6063 🚇 Red Line: Grand 🚌 37, 41

RED ROOF INN CHICAGO DOWNTOWN

www.redroof.com
Rooms are small but well planned in a historic building, some with mini-refrigerator and microwave. The location can't be beat at this price, two blocks off Michigan Avenue in the bustling and usually high-price Streetersville district.

➕ F8 ✉ 162 E. Ontario Street ☎ 312/787-3580; fax 312/787-1299 🚇 Red Line: Grand 🚌 65, 157

WILLOWS HOTEL

www.cityinns.com/willows
A hotel with 55 great-value rooms on a residential street in Lake View, close to the lake, Lincoln Park and numerous bars and restaurants. The building dates from the 1920s and is full of character—the lobby is especially charming, with a fireplace and high windows.

➕ Off map at D1 ✉ 555 W. Surf Street ☎ 773/528-8400 or 800/787-3108 🚇 Brown Line: Diversey 🚌 36

WHERE TO STAY BUDGET HOTELS

Mid-Range Hotels

PRICES

Expect to pay between $150 and $250 for a mid-range hotel.

THE ALLEGRO
www.allegrochicago.com
The 483 rooms are easily the best-price in the Loop. Whimsical interior.
🔲 E9 ✉ 171 W. Randolph Street ☎ 866/672-6143 or 312/236-0123; fax 312/236-3440 🚇 Brown, Orange Lines: Randolph/Wells 🚌 37

BEST WESTERN RIVER NORTH
www.bestwestern.worldexecutive.com
The 145 rooms are good value if unexciting. Plus points are a rooftop pool, exercise room, restaurant and proximity to the nightspots and restaurants of River North.
🔲 F8 ✉ 125 W. Ohio Street ☎ 800/727-0800 or 312/467-0800 🚇 Red Line: Grand 🚌 22

THE BURNHAM
www.burnhamhotel.com
Creative use of the historic Reliance Building has yielded 141 comfortable, smallish rooms with some period details.
🔲 E10 ✉ 1 W. Washington Street ☎ 312/782-1111 or 877/294-9712; fax 312/782-0899 🚇 Blue, Red Lines: Washington 🚌 147, 151

CITY SUITES HOTEL
www.cityinns.com
Most of the 45 rooms are suites—and good value. A lively shopping and nightlife strip is on the doorstep, and loud.
🔲 Off map at C1 ✉ 933 W. Belmont Avenue ☎ 773/404-3400 or 800/248-9108 🚇 Brown, Red Lines: Belmont 🚌 77

COURTYARD BY MARRIOTT
www.marriott.com
The 337 large, comfortable rooms are designed for business travelers. The Loop is adjacent.
🔲 F8 ✉ 30 E. Hubbard Street ☎ 800/228-9290 or 312/329-2500; fax 312/329-0293 🚇 Red Line: Grand 🚌 36

EMBASSY SUITES
www.embassysuiteschicago.com
385 suites in a good location for Michigan Avenue shopping and River North nightlife.

BOOKING

Rooms can be reserved by phone, fax or mail; book as early as possible. A deposit (usually by credit card) equivalent to the nightly rate will ensure your room is held at least until 6pm; inform the hotel if you are arriving later. Credit card is the usual payment method; traveler's checks or cash can be used, but payment might then be expected in advance. The total charge will include the city's 14.9 percent sales and room tax.

Substantial buffet breakfast and a free evening cocktail party included.
🔲 E8 ✉ 600 N. State Street ☎ 312/943-3800 or 800/362-2779 🚇 Red Line: Grand 🚌 36

THE FITZPATRICK CHICAGO HOTEL
A stateside branch of the popular Irish chain, the Fitzgerald provides 140 rooms and suites with canopy beds, cheerful decor and in-room Wi-Fi. A rooftop pool and convivial lobby bar are popular gathering places.
🔲 F7 ✉ 166 E. Superior Street ☎ 312/787-6000 or 800/367-7701; fax: 312/787-6133 🚇 Red Line: Chicago 🚌 66, 151

HILTON CHICAGO
www.chicagohilton.com
More than 1,500 rooms, a pervasive sense of grandeur and the city's largest hotel health club.
🔲 F13 ✉ 720 S. Michigan Avenue ☎ 800/445-8667 or 312/922-4400 🚇 Red Line: Harrison 🚌 1, 3, 4, 6, 146

HOTEL INDIGO CHICAGO
www.ichotelsgroup.com
The InterContinental chain runs this new boutique hotel in an older building on a Gold Coast residential street close to the Magnificent Mile.
🔲 E5 ✉ 1244 N. Dearborn Parkway ☎ 312/787-4980 or 877/846-3446; fax 312/787-4069 🚇 Red Line: Clark/Division 🚌 37, 156

HOTEL MONACO

www.monaco-chicago.com
Stylish striped wallpaper and offbeat colors provide zip to this 192-room boutique hotel in the Loop. Request a room with a window seat to enjoy the view. Free Wi-Fi and a complementary wine reception nightly.

F9 201 N. Wabash Avenue 866/610-0081; fax: 312/960-1883 Brown, Green, Orange Lines: State/Lake 29

HOUSE OF BLUES HOTEL

www.houseofblueshotel.com
Bright colors, busy patterns and folk art liven up this 367-roomer next door to the House of Blues music club. Taped concerts play on elevator video screens.

E9 333 N. Dearborn Street 312/245-0333 or 877/569-3742 Red Line: Grand 22

OLD TOWN CHICAGO

www.oldtownchicago.com
Four suites, sumptuously furnished in a manner befitting the retro art deco style of this town house. In a peaceful residential street in the Old Town.

D5 1442 N. North Park Avenue 312/440-9268; fax 312/440-2378 Brown Line: Sedgwick 72

THE RAPHAEL

www.raphaelchicago.com
Tremendous value in an otherwise costly district,

just off the Magnificent Mile. Most of the 172 rooms are suites with their own refrigerators.

F7 201 E. Delaware Place 800/983-7870 or 312/943-5000; fax 312/943-9483 Red Line: Chicago 145, 146, 147, 151

RENAISSANCE CHICAGO

www.renaissancemarriott.com
The convenient Loop location and the 553 spacious, well-equipped rooms make this a good choice.

E9 1 W. Wacker Drive 888/236-2427 or 312/372-7200; fax 312/372-0093 Red Line: Lake, State; Brown, Green Lines: State 2, 10, 11, 44

SOFITEL CHICAGO WATER TOWER

www.sofitel.com
Striking glass hotel from French hoteliers Sofitel

with good views of the John Hancock and a smart Mag Mile locale. Modern but comfortable furnishings in the rooms.

F7 20 E. Chestnut Street 312/324-4000; fax 312/324-4026 Red Line: Chicago 22, 66

SUTTON PLACE

www.suttonplace.com
In a strikingly modern exterior amid Gold Coast brownstones, 246 comfortable rooms offer hi-speed internet access and climate control.

F6 21 Bellevue Place 312/266-2100 or 866/378-8866; fax 312/266-2141 Red Line: Clarke/Division Any North Michgan Avenue bus

TREMONT HOTEL

www.tremontchicago.com/welcome.asp
This elegant, 130-room, Tudor-style hotel is a stone's throw from Michigan Avenue shopping. Steak house and fitness facility.

F7 100 E. Chestnut Street 312/751-1900 or 800/621-8133; fax 312/751-8691 Red Line: Chicago 145, 146, 147, 151

THE WHITEHALL

www.thewhitehallhotel.com
First opened in the 1920s, this 221-room hotel now has English-style furnishings. Modern amenities; room service.

F7 105 E. Delaware Place 800/948-4255 or 312/944-6300 Red Line: Chicago 145, 146, 147, 151

Luxury Hotels

THE DRAKE

www.thedrakehotel.com
Modeled on an Italian Renaissance palace and opened in 1920, this is a Chicago classic. Some of the 537 rooms have lake views.

F6 140 E. Walton Place 800/553-7253 or 312/787-2200 Red Line: Chicago 145, 146, 147, 151

FAIRMONT HOTEL

www.fairmont.com/chicago
Winning views over Grant Park, the city and the lake; the 672 rooms are comfortable and tasteful. Use of health club.

F9 200 N. Columbus Drive 800/257-2544 or 312/565-8000 Brown, Orange Lines: State, Lake 4

FOUR SEASONS HOTEL CHICAGO

www.fourseasons.com/chicagofs
Excellent service and 343 traditional rooms. Rooftop running track. Roman-style pool and spa.

F7 120 E. Delaware Place 312/280-8800 or 800/819-5053; fax 312/280-1748 Red Line: Chicago 145, 146, 147, 151

HARD ROCK HOTEL

www.hardrockhotelchicago.com
The art deco Carbide and Carbon Building was repurposed as a rock-and-roll theme hotel. The lobby bar draws touring musicians when in town.

F9 230 N. Michigan Avenue 866/ 966-5166 or 312/345-1000; fax 312/345-1012 Brown: Randolph 143, 144, 146, 151

INTERCONTINENTAL CHICAGO

www.chicago.intercontinental.com
A lavish men's club built in 1929 now houses this hotel. The mosaic-tile indoor pool with a terraced deck is a must see. The 800 rooms are split between the historic building and an adjacent modern tower.

F8 505 N. Michigan Avenue 312/944--4100; fax 312/944-1320 Red Line: Grand 143, 144, 145, 146, 151

PARK HYATT CHICAGO

www.parkchicago.hyatt.com
The best rooms, and the hotel's highly regarded NoMI restaurant, peer directly over the historic Water Tower. Photography and fine art complement the modern interiors.

F7 800 N. Michigan Avenue 312/335-1234 Red Line: Chicago 66, 143, 144, 145, 146, 151

THE PENINSULA CHICAGO

www.chicago.peninsula.com
A gilded link in the Asia-based chain, the Peninsula Chicago pampers guests with a gleaming lobby, top-floor lap pool with skyline views and room controls for temperature, curtains and valet notices from a bedside console.

F7 108 E. Superior Street 866/288-8889 or 312/337-2888; fax 312/751-2888 Red Line: Chicago 143, 144, 145, 146, 151

RITZ-CARLTON CHICAGO

www.fourseasons.com/chicagorc
Whim-catering hotel popular with celebrities passing through town. The restaurant is a stand out. Shoppers like the locale just off Michigan Avenue at Water Tower Place.

F7 160 E. Pearson Street 800/819-5053 or 312/266-1000; fax. 312/266-1194 Red Line: Chicago 143, 144, 145, 146, 151

Use this section to familiarize yourself with travel to and within Chicago. Planning can help save money: the multiday visitor's pass allowing unlimited trips on the mass transit system is sold in advance.

Planning Ahead

When To Go

June, July and August are the busiest months, but the weather can be tryingly hot. May, September and October are better months to visit, with fewer crowds and warm but less extreme weather. Events and festivals take place year-round. Major conventions in August, September and October cause hotel space to be scarce.

> **TIME**
>
> Chicago is one hour behind New York, two hours ahead of Los Angeles and six hours behind the UK.

AVERAGE DAILY MAXIMUM TEMPERATURES											
JAN	FEB	MAR	APR	MAY	JUN	JUL	AUG	SEP	OCT	NOV	DEC
22°F	26°F	37°F	49°F	59°F	69°F	74°F	72°F	65°F	53°F	40°F	27°F
-6°C	-3°C	3°C	9°C	15°C	21°C	23°C	22°C	18°C	12°C	4°C	-3°C

Spring (mid-March to May) Very changeable; sometimes snow, sometimes sun, but generally mild.

Summer (June to mid-September) Varies from warm to very hot, sometimes uncomfortably so with high humidity.

Autumn (mid-September to October) Though changeable, it is often mild with sunny days.

Winter (November to mid-March) Often very cold with heavy snow and strong winds. Winds can be strong any time and particularly cold when, usually in winter, they come from the north.

WHAT'S ON

January/February *Chinese New Year*: In Chinatown.

March *St. Patrick's Day*: The city turns green, and there's a parade through the Loop.

April *Baseball season* opens. *Chicago Antiques and Fine Art Fair*.

May *Polish Constitution Day* (May 7): Chicago's Polish Americans celebrate with a parade and events focusing on Polish culture.

Wright Plus: See inside Oak Park homes designed by Frank Lloyd Wright.

June *Chicago Blues Festival*: Local and international artists perform in Grant Park.

Printer's Row Book Fair: Used-book shops host events.

Chicago Gospel Festival: Gospel music in Grant Park.

July *Taste of Chicago*: a feeding frenzy; in the 11 days leading up to July 4, thousands sample dishes from city restaurants.

Independence Day (Jul 4): Special events such as fireworks displays, the largest taking place in Grant Park.

August *Ravinia Festival* (mid-Jun to Labor Day): Two months of the Chicago Symphony Orchestra, pop, folk and rock music, with picnicking on the lawns.

Chicago Air & Water Show: Spectacular stunts performed off North Avenue Beach.

September *Chicago Jazz Festival*: Jazz stars headline free concerts in Grant Park.

October *Chicago Marathon*.

November/December *Festival of Lights*: Lights along the Magnificent Mile.

Chicago Online

www.ci.chi.il.us

The city government website Chicagoans use this to pay their bills and make complaints, but it holds plenty of interest to visitors.

www.choosechicago.com

Part of the above, but aimed more squarely at visitors. Most sections comprise links to other organizations, but it's a good start point for annual events and cultural activities.

www.chicagotribune.com

The online version of Chicago's biggest circulation daily newspaper requiring (free) registration. Its listings sister site, metromix is free and does not require registration.

www.suntimes.com

The online version of Chicago's tabloid daily newspaper, with full access to news and feature stories, plus sports and, if you should want it, access to its advertisements.

www.chicagoreader.com

The website of the city's long-established alternative weekly newspaper, the *Chicago Reader*, with a different slant on city affairs and its own recommendations for entertainment.

www.newcitychicago.com

A more recent alternative weekly, *New City Chicago* is slicker and snappier in style than the Reader, but sometimes less satisfying.

www.metromix.com

Offshoot of the *Chicago Tribune* with informative listings, covering events, museums, dining, nightlife and more.

www.urchicago.com

Opinionated takes on the Chicago clubbing scene and much more about the city from a late-night perspective.

PRIME TRAVEL SITES

www.fodors.com

A complete travel-planning site. Research prices and the weather; reserve air tickets, cars and rooms; ask questions (and get answers) from fellow visitors; and find links to other sites.

www.transitchicago.com

The website of the Chicago Transit Authority explains all there is to know about using the city's buses and El trains, the fares and ticket types, with route maps that can be downloaded and lots more.

INTERNET CAFÉS

Windy City Cyber Café

Computers plus coffee, tea and artwork by Wicker Park locals.

🕂 C4 ✉ 2246 W. North Avenue ☎ 773/384-6470 🕐 Mon–Fri 8–10, Sat–Sun 8–10 💵 $6 per hour

Screenz Digital Universe

Broadband connections and screened-off workstations with all the appropriate software.

🕂 C1 ✉ 2717 N. Clark Street ☎ 773/348-9300 🕐 Daily 10am–midnight 💵 $10–$12 per hour

Getting There

INSURANCE

It is vital to have coverage for medical expenses, as well as theft, baggage loss, trip cancellation and accidents. Check your insurance coverage and buy a supplementary policy as needed.

ENTRY REQUIREMENTS

UK citizens require a machine-readable passport, valid for at least six months. Passports issued on or after October 26 2004 must include a biometric identifier; UK passports already issued will still qualify for visa-free travel, as will those of other countries in the visa-waiver scheme. Check the current situation before you leave (US Embassy visa information ☎ 0891 200-2900; www.usembassy.org).

AIRPORTS

Chicago's O'Hare International Airport is 17 miles (27km) northwest of the Loop and takes all international flights and most domestic flights. Midway Airport, 8 miles (13km) southwest of the Loop, is a quieter alternative for domestic flights.

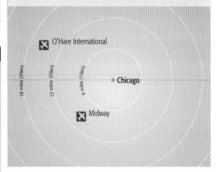

FROM O'HARE INTERNATIONAL AIRPORT

For information on O'Hare International Airport ☎ 773/686-2000; www.ohare.com.
Continental Airport Express (☎ 312/454-800 or 800/654-7871; www.airportexpress.com) runs minibuses between O'Hare and the Loop every 10–15 minutes 6am–11.30pm (fare $25; journey time 60 minutes). Pick them up from outside the arrivals terminal. Make a reservation for the return trip from your hotel to the airport.

Chicago Transit Authority (☎ 888/968-7282; www.transitchicago.com) operates Blue Line trains between O'Hare and the Loop (24 hours; journey time 45 minutes; fare $2). Follow the signs from the arrivals hall to the station. However, it is safer to take a taxi late at night from either airport. Taxis wait outside the arrivals terminal and the fare to the Loop or nearby hotels is about $35–$40.

ARRIVING AT MIDWAY AIRPORT

For information about Midway Airport ☎ 773/838-0600; www.ohare.com/midway/

home.asp. Continental Airport Express runs minibuses to the Loop every 15 minutes 6am–10.30pm (fare around $6; journey time 60 minutes). Pick them up from outside Door 3 on the lower level.

Chicago Transit Authority runs Orange Line trains to the Loop from 3.55am–12.55am, beginning at 4.35am on Saturday and 5.35am on Sunday and holidays, (fare $2; journey time 30 minutes). Taxis wait at the arrivals terminal. The fare to the Loop or nearby hotels is approximately $30.

ARRIVING BY BUS

Greyhound buses (☎ 800/229-9424; 312/408-5800; www.greyhound.com) arrive at 630 W. Harrison Street, six blocks southwest of the Loop. MegaBus (www.megabus.com), which serves eight Midwestern cities with budget-priced fares, stops at Union Station on the east side of S. Canal Street, between Jackson Boulevard and Adams Street.

ARRIVING BY CAR

Chicago has good Interstate access: I-80 and I-90 are the major east–west routes; I-55 and I-57 arrive from the south. I-94 runs through the city linking the north and south suburbs. To reach the Loop from O'Hare airport use I-90/94. From Midway airport take I-55, linking with the northbound I-90/94 for the Loop. These journeys take 45–90 minutes and 30–60 minutes respectively depending on traffic and weather. Avoid the rush hours, 7–9am and 4–7pm.

ARRIVING BY TRAIN

Amtrak trains (Information ☎ 800/ 872-7245 or 312/655-2111; www.amtrak.com) use Chicago's Union Station, junction of W. Adams and S. Canal streets, two blocks west of the Loop.

CHICAGO GREETER

The Chicago Office of Tourism's Department of Cultural Affairs runs a program to match volunteer residents with inquiring visitors. Chicago Greeters won't meet you at the airport, nor even on the day that you arrive, but by prior arrangement will spend two to four hours showing you around the city and providing an insider's point of view. The service is free but requires a seven-day advance registration via the website www.chicagogreeter.com. Greeters will escort one to six visitors on the itinerary of their choice ranging from outings themed to food or history or itineraries that look at a specific neighborhood.

Getting Around

DRIVING IN CHICAGO

Driving in the city is stressful: use public transportation. Many hotels have parking lots, otherwise overnight parking is difficult and very costly. During the day, street parking is often limited to two hours; spaces in the Loop are near impossible to find.

VISITORS WITH DISABILITIES

Legislation aimed at improving access for visitors with disabilities in Chicago means that all recently built structures have to provide disabled access; the newer they are, the stricter the rules. Many older buildings, including most hotels, have been converted to ensure they comply. Both airports are accessible, as are many CTA buses and El stations. For details log onto www.transitchicago.com/maps/accessible.html

Much of Chicago can be explored on foot. To travel between neighborhoods use the network of buses and El (elevated) trains, which travel above and below ground. El trains operate 24-hours a day, but using trains or buses late at night can be dangerous. Best value over many journeys are the Visitor Pass tickets valid for 1–5 days (cost $5–$18). Buy them from the airport CTA stations, from major museums and the Visitor Information (for information C1-888/968-7282). Tokens, cash and multi-use plastic cards can also be used. Taxis wait outside hotels, conference halls and major El stations, or can be hailed.

● Using trains or buses at night can be dangerous.

● Metra commuter trains are best for visiting some areas.

● For information on the El and buses: Chicago Transit Authority ☎ 888/968-7282; Metra ☎ 312/322-6777 (🕐 Mon–Fri 8–5), otherwise 312/836-7000.

THE EL

● Fare: $2. Transfer to a different line (or to a bus) within two hours: 25¢ (free within Loop). A second transfer within the same two hours is free. Children 7–11 ride for 85c, $1 with transfer. Kids under age 6 travel free.

● Plastic transit cards are the simplest way to pay fares. Cash is an alternative. Cards are dispensed in exchange for cash from automated machines at train stations with a minimum value of $2. Replenish existing cards with more cash as needed at the same machines.

● Visitor passes valid for 1 day ($5), 2 days ($9), 3 days ($12) or 5 days ($18) permit unlimited rides on buses and trains. The pass activates the first time you use it and is good for the consecutive number of calendar days shown on the front of the pass. Order them before you arrive at the CTA website (www.transitchicago.com) or buy them at many hotels, Chicago visitor centers and O'Hare and Midway CTA stations.

- Stations have fare booths or automatic ticket machines.
- Seven color-coded lines run through the city and converge on the Loop.
- On weekdays 6am–7pm, some trains stop only at alternate stations, plus all major stations. Station announcements will alert you to the change.
- Most trains run 24 hours; frequency is reduced on weekends and late evenings. The Brown, Green and Orange Lines suspend service between roughly 2am and 5am.
- Some stations are closed weekends.

BUSES

- Fare: $1.75 with a transit card, $2 with cash. Transfer to a different route (or to the El) within two hours: 25¢. Second transfer as for the El.
- As for the El, plastic transit cards are the simplest way to pay fares. They are sold at CTA train stations.

SCHEDULE AND MAP INFORMATION

- CTA maps showing El and bus routes are available from El station fare booths.
- Bus routes are shown at stops.
- The CTA website (www.transitchicago.com) contains all schedules and maps and offers directions on how to get to popular tourist attractions under "Top Transit Tips."

TAXIS

- Fares are $2.25 for the first 0.9 miles and 20c for each additional 0.9 miles or 36 seconds elapsed waiting time, whichever comes first. The second additional passenger costs $1 and each additional passenger after that costs 50c. Midway- and O'Hare-bound trips cost an extra $1.
- Hotel, restaurant and nightclub staff will order a taxi on request; or you can phone Checker ☎ 312/243-2537; Flash ☎ 773/561-4444 or Yellow ☎ 312/829-4222.

GOING BY WATER

In spring and summer the Wendella Riverbus (☎ 312/337-1446; www.wendellariverbus.com) offers ferry service from 7am to, roughly, sundown. Catch it as one of four stops along the Chicago River: Madison Street., La Salle Street, Michigan Avenue and North Pier. A single one-way ticket costs $2, a bargain tour of the city by water.

MAPPING CHICAGO

Most of Chicago is laid out on a grid system with ground zero at State, which runs north–south, and Madison, east–west, in the Loop. Each block number changes by 100 with eight blocks equaling roughly one mile (1.6km). For instance, 800 N. State Street means the location is eight blocks north of the baseline intersection, while 110 E. Madison lies on the second block east of it. Even number addresses belong to the north or west side of a street; odd numbers mean the location is on the south or east side of a street.

Essential Facts

VISA AND TRAVEL INSURANCE

Visitors from the UK can spend up to six months in the United States without a visa, showing only a passport. The British Embassy in the US posts updated visa requirements at its website, www.britainusa.com. Some travelers may want to consider buying travel insurance, which will cover trip cancellation, lost baggage and car rentals.

MONEY

Dollar bills (notes) come in denominations of $1, $5, $10, $20, $50 and $100; coins are 25¢ (a quarter), 10¢ (a dime), 5¢ (a nickel) and 1¢ (a penny).

5 dollars

10 dollars

50 dollars

100 dollars

CUSTOMS REGULATIONS

● Duty-free allowances include 32fl oz alcoholic spirits or wine (no one under 21 may bring alcohol into the US), 200 cigarettes or 50 cigars, and up to $100-worth of gifts.
● Some medication bought over the counter abroad may be prescription-only in the US and may be confiscated. Bring a doctor's certificate for essential medication.
● It is forbidden to bring food, seeds and plants into the US.

ELECTRICITY

● The supply is 110 volts; 60 cycles AC current.
● US appliances use two-prong plugs. European appliances require an adaptor.

ETIQUETTE

● Smoking is banned in all public buildings and transportation. It is also banned or restricted in many hotels and restaurants.
● Tipping is voluntary, but the following are usually expected: 15 percent-plus in restaurants; 15–20 percent for taxis; $1 per bag for a hotel porter.

INTERNATIONAL NEWSAGENTS

● Overseas newspapers and magazines can be found at Barnes & Noble and Borders Books & Music stores.

MEDICAL TREATMENT

● For doctors, ask hotel staff or the nonemergency Medical Referral Service ☎ 312/670-2550.
● In an emergency go to a hospital with a 24-hour emergency room, such as Northwestern Memorial Hospital at 250 E. Erie Street ☎ 312/926-2000.
● The Chicago Dental Association ☎ 312/836-7300 will refer you to a dentist in your area.

MEDICINES

● Pharmacies are listed in *Yellow Pages*. Visitors from Europe will find many familiar

medicines under unfamiliar names. Some drugs, available over the counter at home, are prescription-only in the US.

● If you use medication bring a supply (but note the warning given in Customs Regulations, ▷ 120). If you intend to buy prescription drugs in the US, bring a note from your doctor.

● Late-night pharmacies in the city include Walgreen's ✉ 757 N. Michigan Avenue ☎ 312/664-4000 🕐 24 hours.
Osco Drug has a toll-free number ☎ 888/443-5701 giving the location of its nearest 24-hour branch.

MONEY MATTERS

● Most banks have ATMs, which accept credit cards registered in other countries that are linked to the Cirrus or Plus networks. Ensure your personal identification number is valid in the US: four- and six-figure numbers are usual.

● Credit cards are widely accepted.

● US dollar traveler's checks function like cash in most shops; $20 and $50 denominations are most useful. Seeking to exchange these (or foreign currency) at a bank can be difficult and commissions can be high.

● A 9 percent sales tax is added to marked retail prices, except on groceries and prescription drugs.

NEWSPAPERS AND MAGAZINES

● Major daily newspapers are the *Chicago Tribune* and the tabloid *Chicago Sun-Times* (international, national and local stories).

● Best of several free weeklies is the *Chicago Reader*. The glossy *Time Out Chicago* covers the same ground for a fee at newsstands.

● Glossy monthly magazines such as *Chicago* reflect the interests of the well-heeled Chicagoan. *Windy City Times* is pitched at gays and lesbians.

● Free magazines such as *Where Chicago*, found in hotel lobbies, are aimed at tourists.

TOURIST OFFICES

Visitor centers are inside the Chicago Water Tower ✉ 163 E. Pearson Street ☎ 312/744-2400, at the Chicago Cultural Center ✉ 77 E. Randolph Street ☎ 312/744-2400, and at Illinois Market Place ✉ Navy Pier, 700 E. Grand Avenue. All are open daily but may close on holidays.

NATIONAL HOLIDAYS

● New Year's Day (Jan 1)
● Martin Luther King Day (third Mon in Jan)
● President's Day (third Mon in Feb)
● Memorial Day (last Mon in May)
● Independence Day (Jul 4)
● Labor Day (first Mon in Sep)
● Columbus Day (second Mon in Oct)
● Veteran's Day (Nov 11)
● Thanksgiving Day (fourth Thu in Nov)
● Christmas Day (Dec 25)

EMERGENCY PHONE NUMBERS

● Fire, police or ambulance ☎ 911 (no money required)
● Rape Crisis Hotline ☎ 888/293-2080

LOST PROPERTY

● O'Hare International Airport ☎ 800/832-6352
● Items lost in a cab; Department of Consumer Services ☎ 312/744-4006
● The El and buses: Chicago Transit Authority ☎ 888/ 968-7282; Metra ◎ Daily 7.45am–1am ☎ 312/836-7000

RADIO AND TV

Radio
● Classical: WFMT 98.7FM
● Country: WUSN 99.5FM
● Jazz: WNUA 95.5FM
● National Public Radio: WBEZ 91.5FM
● News: WBBM 780AM
● Rock: WCKG 105.9FM
● R&B: WGCI 107.5FM
● Talk radio and local sports: WGN 820AM; WSCR 670AM

Television
● The main Chicago TV channels are 2 WBBM (CBS), 5 WMAQ (NBC), 7 WLS (ABC), 9 WGN (local WB affiliate), 11 WTTW (PBS), 32 WFLD (Fox).

OPENING HOURS

● Stores: Mon–Sat from 9 or 10 until 5 or 6. Most stores are also open Sun noon–5. Department stores and malls keep longer hours; bookshops may open in the evenings.
● Banks: Mon–Fri from 8 or 9 to 4 or 5, with some branches open later once a week.

POST OFFICES

● Minimum charges for sending a postcard or letter overseas are 75¢ and 84¢ respectively.
● To find the nearest post office, look in the phone book or ask at your hotel. Most open Mon–Fri 8.30–5, Sat 8.30–1 ☎ 312/654-3789.

SENSIBLE PRECAUTIONS

● By day, the Loop and major areas of interest to visitors are relatively safe. Some tourist sites involve journeys through unwelcoming areas; be especially wary if traveling through the South Side and West Side. Discuss your itinerary with hotel staff and heed their advice.
● After dark, stay in established nightlife areas. River North and River West, Rush and Division streets, and Lake View/Wrigleyville are fairly safe if you use common-sense precautions. Public transportation is generally safe between these areas, but be cautious.
● Neighborhoods can change character within a few blocks. Stick to safe, busy streets.
● Carry shoulder bags strapped across your chest, and keep your wallet in your front trouser pocket or chest pocket. Keep your belongings within sight and within reach.
● Store valuables in your hotel's safe and never carry more money than you need.
● Lost traveler's checks are easy to replace— read the instrucions when you buy them and keep the instructions handy (separate from the checks).
● Replacing a stolen passport is tricky and begins with a visit or phone call to your nearest consular office.
● Report any item stolen to the nearest police precinct (see the phone book). It is unlikely

that stolen goods will be recovered, but the police will fill in the forms your insurance company needs.

SOLO VISITORS
● Solo visitors, including women, are not unusual.
● Women may encounter unwanted attention and, after dark, should avoid being out alone when not in established nightlife areas. Wait for a cab inside a club or restaurant, or where staff can see you.

STUDENT VISITORS
● An International Student Identity Card (ISIC) reduces admission to many museums and other attractions.
● Anyone aged under 21 is forbidden to buy or drink alcohol and may be denied admission to some nightclubs.

TELEPHONES
● Public telephones are found in the street and in public buildings. Local calls cost 50¢.
● Calls from hotel rooms are usually more expensive than those from public phones.
● Many businesses have toll-free numbers, prefixed with 800, 866 or 888.
● Most US phones use touch-tone dialing, enabling callers to access extensions directly.
● To call Chicago from the UK dial 001 followed by the full number. To call the UK from Chicago dial 011 and omit the first zero from the area code.

TOILETS
● Most department stores, malls and hotel lobbies have adequate toilets.

TRAVELING WITH CHILDREN
Chicago is a destination that welcomes children. Classic sights like the Sears Tower Observatory, Navy Pier, Shedd Aquarium, Field Museum, Museum of Science and Industry and the Chicago Children's Museum delight all ages, but especially kids. Furthermore, adults don't have to sacrifice their own interests to those of a child. The Art Institute of Chicago runs an outstanding visitor's program for children, including a tour and art-working workshop on weekends year-round and more commonly in summer. The Jazz Showcase offers family-friendly matinees every Sunday. The fountain in Millennium Park is a popular spot for kids to play in summer in the water while families tour the grounds. When rest is required for little legs go passive sightseeing by riding the El or taking a water taxi.

CONSULATES		
Germany	✉ 676 N. Michigan Avenue, Suite 3200	☎ 312/202-0480
Ireland	✉ 400 N. Michigan Avenue, Suite 911	☎ 312/337-1868
UK	✉ 400 N. Michigan Avenue, Suite 1300	☎ 312/970-3800

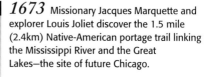

Timeline

NEED TO KNOW TIMELINE

WINDY CITY

In 1893 Chicago hosted the World's Columbian Exposition. The hyperbole of business leaders caused one journalist to describe Chicago as "the windy city," an enduring epithet.

THE HAYMARKET RIOT

Heavy-handed police tactics in a series of labor disputes prompted a group of German-born anarchists to organize a protest rally on May 4 1886, in Haymarket Square. A bomb thrown from the crowd exploded among the police lines; the explosion and the police use of firearms killed seven people and wounded 150. Seven anarchists received death sentences. In 1893, a full pardon was granted to three imprisoned anarchists, due to the lack of evidence linking any anarchists to the bomb.

1673 Missionary Jacques Marquette and explorer Louis Joliet discover the 1.5 mile (2.4km) Native-American portage trail linking the Mississippi River and the Great Lakes—the site of future Chicago.

1779–81 Trapper and trader Jean-Baptiste Point du Sable, a Haitian, becomes the first non-native settler.

1812 Fort Dearborn, one of several forts protecting trade routes, is attacked by Native Americans.

1830 Chicago is selected as the site of a canal linking the Great Lakes and the Mississippi.

1870 Chicago's population reaches 330,000 from 30,000 in 1850. Many arrivals are Irish, who find work building the railways.

1871 The Great Fire kills 300 people.

1894 A strike at the Pullman rail company unites black and white workers for the first time.

1906 Upton Sinclair's novel *The Jungle* focuses national attention on the conditions endured by workers in the notorious Union Stockyards.

1908 Chicago Cubs win baseball's World Series for a second successive year.

1914 With World War I, Chicago's black population increases further, as African-Americans from the Deep South move north to industrial jobs.

1919–33 Prohibition. Chicago's transport links make it a natural place for alcohol manufacture and distribution. Armed crime mobs thrive.

1950s In South Side clubs, rhythmic and electrified Chicago blues evolves.

1955 Richard J. Daley is elected mayor and dominates Chicago political life for 21 years.

1968 Police attack Anti-Vietnam War protesters in Grant Park during the Democratic National Convention.

1974 Completion of Sears Tower, the world's tallest building until 1996.

1980s DJs at Chicago's Warehouse nightclub create house music.

1992 A collapsing wall causes the Chicago River to flood the Loop.

2003 The runway at Meigs Field airport s is bull-dozed without warning by order of the mayor.

2007 The Chicago River is dyed green for the 51st time in honor of St. Patrick's Day.

GANGSTERS

Intended to encourage sobriety and family life, Prohibition (1919–33) provided a great stimulus to organized crime. The exploits of Chicago-based gangsters such as Al Capone became legendary. Though depicted frequently on films and TV, shoot-outs between rival gangs were rare. An exception was the 1929 Valentine's Day Massacre, when Capone's gang eliminated their archrivals in a hail of machine-gun fire. Wealthy enough to bribe corruptible politicians and police, the gangsters seemed invincible, but the gangster era—though not necessarily the gangs—ended with Capone's imprisonment in 1931 and the repeal of Prohibition.

From the left: Directions to the Clarke House; a baseball game in progress at Wrigley Field; an old copy of the Chicago Daily Tribune; *the Chicago skyline from the Sears Tower*

Index

INDEX

Chicago's
25 BEST

WRITTEN BY Mick Sinclair
ADDITIONAL WRITING Elaine Glusac
DESIGN CONCEPT AND DESIGN WORK Kate Harling
INDEXER Marie Lorimer
REVIEWING EDITOR Jacinta O'Halloran
SERIES EDITOR Paul Mitchell

ISBN 978-1-4000-1760-7

FIFTH EDITION

IMPORTANT TIP
Time inevitably brings changes, so always confirm prices, travel facts, and other perishable information when it matters. Although Fodor's cannot accept responsibility for errors, you can use this guide in the confidence that we have taken every care to ensure its accuracy.

SPECIAL SALES
This book is available for special discounts for bulk purchases for sales promotions or premiums. Special editions, including personalized covers, excerpts of existing books, and corporate imprints, can be created in large quantities for special needs. For more information, write to Special Markets/Premium Sales, 1745 Broadway, MD 6–2, New York, NY 10019 or email specialmarkets@randomhouse.com.

First published 1997
Colour separation by Keenes
Printed and bound by Leo, China
10 9 8 7 6 5 4 3 2 1

A02815
Maps in this title produced from mapping © MAIRDUMONT / Falk Verlag 2006 and map data © Global Mapping (www.globalmapping.uk.com)
Transport map © Communicarta Ltd, UK

The Automobile Association wishes to thank the following photographers, companies and picture libraries for their assistance in the preparation of this book.

Abbreviations for the picture credits are as follows – (t) top; (b) bottom; (l) left; (r) right; (c) center; (AA) AA World Travel Library

IFC i AA/C Sawyer; **IFC ii** AA/C Sawyer; **IFC iii** AA/C Sawyer; **IFC iv** AA/C Sawyer; **IFC v** AA/C Sawyer; **IFC vi** AA/C Sawyer; **IFC vii** AA/P Wood; **IFC viii** Art Institute of Chicago; **IFC ix** Shedd Aquarium; **IFC x** AA/P Wood; **1** AA/C Sawyer; **2** AA/C Sawyer; **3** AA/C Sawyer; **4** AA/C Sawyer; **4c** AA/C Sawyer; **5t** AA/C Sawyer; **5b** AA/P Wilson; **6t** AA/C Sawyer; **6cl** AA/C Sawyer; **6ct** AA/P Wilson; **6bl** AA/C Sawyer; **6br** AA/C Sawyer; **7t** AA/C Sawyer; **7cl** AA/C Sawyer; **7cr** AA/C Sawyer; **7bl** AA/C Sawyer; **7bc** AA/C Sawyer; **7br** AA/C Sawyer; **8** AA/C Sawyer; **9** AA/C Sawyer; **10t** AA/C Sawyer; **10ct** AA/C Sawyer; **10c** AA/A Mockford & N Bonetti; **10cb** AA/C Sawyer; **10/11** AA/C Sawyer; **11t** AA/C Sawyer; **11ct** AA/C Sawyer; **11c** AA/C Sawyer; **11cb** AA/C Sawyer; **12t** AA/C Sawyer; **12b** AA/C Sawyer; **13t** AA/C Sawyer; **13ctt** AA/C Saywer; **13ct** AA/C Sawyer; **13c** AA/C Sawyer; **13cb** AA/C Sawyer; **13b** AA/C Sawyer; **14t** AA/C Sawyer; **14ctt** AA/C Sawyer; **14ct** AA/C Sawyer; **14c** AA/C Sawyer; **14cb** AA/C Sawyer; **14b** AA/C Sawyer; **15** AA/C Sawyer; **16t** AA/C Sawyer; **16ct** AA/C Sawyer; **16cb** AA/C Sawyer; **16b** AA/C Sawyer; **17t** AA/C Sawyer; **17ct** AA/C Sawyer; **17c** Digital Vision; **17cb** AA/C Sawyer; **17b** AA/C Sawyer; **18t** AA/C Sawyer; **18ct** AA/C Sawyer; **18c** AA/C Sawyer; **18cb** AA/C Sawyer; **18b** AA/C Sawyer; **19t** AA/C Sawyer; **19ct** AA/C Sawyer; **19c** AA/C Sawyer; **19cb** AA/C Sawyer; **19b** AA/C Sawyer; **20/21** AA/P Wilson; **24l** AA/C Sawyer; **24r** AA/C Sawyer; **25l** AA/C Sawyer; **25r** AA/C Sawyer; **26l** AA/C Sawyer; **26r** AA/C Sawyer; **27l** AA/C Sawyer; **27r** AA/C Sawyer; **28t** AA/C Sawyer; **28bl** AA/P Wilson; **28br** AA/C Sawyer; **29** AA/C Sawyer; **30t** AA/P Wilson; **30bl** AA/P Wilson; **30br** AA/P Wilson; **31t** AA/P Wilson; **31bl** Museum of Contemporary Art; **31br** AA/P Wilson; **32** AA/P Wilson; **33** AA/A Mockford & N Bonetti; **34** AA/C Sawyer; **35** Digital Vision; **36** AA/C Sawyer; **37** AA/C Sawyer; **38** AA/C Sawyer; **39** AA/C Sawyer; **42l** AA/P Wilson; **42/43t** AA/P Wilson; **42/43c** AA/P Wilson; **43cl** AA/P Wilson; **43cr** AA/P Wilson; **44** Art Institute of Chicago; **45** Art Institute of Chicago; **46t** AA/P Wilson; **46cl** AA/P Wilson; **46cr** AA/P Wilson; **46/47** AA/C Sawyer; **48t** Shedd Aquarium; **48b** Shedd Aquarium; **49l** Shedd Aquarium; **49t** Shedd Aquarium; **50l** AA/C Sawyer; **50r** AA/C Sawyer; **51t** AA/P Wilson; **51bl** AA/P Wilson; **51br** AA/P Wilson; **52** AA/P Wilson; **53t** AA/Slide File; **53c** AA/C Sawyer; **54** Imagestate; **55** AA/C Sawyer; **58** AA/P Wilson; **59l** AA/P Wilson; **59r** AA/C Sawyer; **60l** Signature Room at the 95th, Chicago; **60r** Signature at the 95th, Chicago; **61l** AA/C Sawyer; **61r** AA/C Sawyer; **62t** AA/C Sawyer; **62cl** AA/C Sawyer; **62cr** AA/C Sawyer; **63t** AA/C Sawyer; **63cl** AA/C Sawyer; **63cr** AA/C Sawyer; **64** AA/C Sawyer; **64/65t** AA/C Sawyer; **64/65c** AA/C Sawyer; **65** AA/C Sawyer; **66l** AA/C Sawyer; **66r** AA/P Wilson; **67l** AA/C Sawyer; **67c** AA/C Sawyer; **67r** AA/C Sawyer; **68l** AA/C Sawyer; **68c** AA/C Sawyer; **68r** AA/C Sawyer; **69t** AA/P Wilson; **69bl** Chicago Children's Museum; **69br** AA/P Wilson; **70t** AA/P Wilson; **70bl** International Museum of Surgical Sciences; **70br** AA/C Sawyer; **71t** AA/P Wilson; **71b** AA/P Wilson; **72t** AA/P Wilson; **72bl** AA/C Sawyer; **72br** AA/P Wilson; **73** AA/P Wilson; **74** AA/S McBride; **75** AA/M Chaplow; **76** Digital Vision; **77** AA/C Sawyer; **78** AA/C Sawyer; **79** AA/C Sawyer; **80** Photodisc; **81** AA/C Sawyer; **84l** AA/C Sawyer; **84r** AA/C Sawyer; **85l** AA/P Wilson; **85r** AA/P Wilson; **86l** AA/C Sawyer; **86r** AA/C Sawyer; **87l** AA/C Sawyer; **87r** Glessner House; **88l** Museum of Science and Industry; **88/89t** Museum of Science and Industry; **88c** Museum of Science and Industry; **88/89c** Museum of Science and Industry; **89t** Museum of Science and Industry; **89r** Museum of Science and Industry; **90t** AA/P Wilson; **90b** AA/C Sawyer; **91t** AA/P Wilson; **91bl** Smart Museum; **91br** AA/P Wilson; **92** AA/P Wilson; **93** AA/C Sawyer; **94** AA/C Sawyer; **95** AA/C Sawyer; **98** AA/C Sawyer; **99l** AA/C Sawyer; **99r** AA/C Sawyer; **100** AA/C Sawyer; **101** The Frank Lloyd Wright Preservation Trust – photographer Tim Long; **102t** AA/P Wilson; **102bl** AA/P Wilson; **102br** AA/C Sawyer; **103** AA/C Sawyer; **104** Digital Vision; **105** Photodisc; **106** AA/C Sawyer; **107** AA/C Sawyer; **108t** AA/C Sawyer; **108c** AA/C Sawyer; **108cb** AA/S McBride; **109** AA/C Sawyer; **110** AA/C Sawyer; **111** AA/C Sawyer; **112** AA/C Sawyer; **113** AA/C Sawyer; **114** AA/C Sawyer; **115** AA/C Sawyer; **116** AA/C Sawyer; **117** AA/C Sawyer; **118** AA/C Sawyer; **119t** AA/C Sawyer; **119b** AA/C Sawyer; **120t** AA/C Sawyer; **120b** MRI Bankers Guide; **121** AA/C Sawyer; **122t** AA/C Sawyer; **122b** AA/C Sawyer; **123t** AA/C Sawyer; **123b** AA/C Sawyer; **124t** AA/C Sawyer; **124bl** AA/P Wilson; **124br** AA/C Sawyer; **125t** AA/C Sawyer; **125bl** AA/P Wilson; **125br** AA/C Sawyer.

Every effort has been made to trace the copyright holders, and we apologise in advance for any unintentional omissions or errors. We would be please to apply any corrections in any following edition of this publication.